Getting Started with Beautiful Soup

Build your own web scraper and learn all about web scraping with Beautiful Soup

Vineeth G. Nair

[PACKT] open source*
PUBLISHING   community experience distilled

BIRMINGHAM - MUMBAI

Getting Started with Beautiful Soup

Copyright © 2014 Packt Publishing

All rights reserved. No part of this book may be reproduced, stored in a retrieval system, or transmitted in any form or by any means, without the prior written permission of the publisher, except in the case of brief quotations embedded in critical articles or reviews.

Every effort has been made in the preparation of this book to ensure the accuracy of the information presented. However, the information contained in this book is sold without warranty, either express or implied. Neither the author, nor Packt Publishing, and its dealers and distributors will be held liable for any damages caused or alleged to be caused directly or indirectly by this book.

Packt Publishing has endeavored to provide trademark information about all of the companies and products mentioned in this book by the appropriate use of capitals. However, Packt Publishing cannot guarantee the accuracy of this information.

First published: January 2014

Production Reference: 1170114

Published by Packt Publishing Ltd.

Livery Place
35 Livery Street
Birmingham B3 2PB, UK.

ISBN 978-1-78328-955-4

www.packtpub.com

Cover Image by Mohamed Raoof (raoofpmajeed@gmail.com)

Credits

Author
Vineeth G. Nair

Reviewers
John J. Czaplewski
Christian S. Perone
Zhang Xiang

Acquisition Editor
Nikhil Karkal

Senior Commissioning Editor
Kunal Parikh

Commissioning Editor
Manasi Pandire

Technical Editors
Novina Kewalramani
Pooja Nair

Copy Editor
Janbal Dharmaraj

Project Coordinator
Jomin Varghese

Proofreader
Maria Gould

Indexer
Hemangini Bari

Graphics
Sheetal Aute
Abhinash Sahu

Production Coordinator
Adonia Jones

Cover Work
Adonia Jones

About the Author

Vineeth G. Nair completed his bachelors in Computer Science and Engineering from Model Engineering College, Cochin, Kerala. He is currently working with Oracle India Pvt. Ltd. as a Senior Applications Engineer.

He developed an interest in Python during his college days and began working as a freelance programmer. This led him to work on several web scraping projects using Beautiful Soup. It helped him gain a fair level of mastery on the technology and a good reputation in the freelance arena. He can be reached at vineethgnair.mec@gmail.com. You can visit his website at www.kochi-coders.com.

> My sincere thanks to Leonard Richardson, the primary author of Beautiful Soup. I would like to thank my friends and family for their great support and encouragement for writing this book. My special thanks to Vijitha S. Menon, for always keeping my spirits up, providing valuable comments, and showing me the best ways to bring this book up. My sincere thanks to all the reviewers for their suggestions, corrections, and points of improvement.
>
> I extend my gratitude to the team at Packt Publishing who helped me in making this book happen.

About the Reviewers

John J. Czaplewski is a Madison, Wisconsin-based mapper and web developer who specializes in web-based mapping, GIS, and data manipulation and visualization. He attended the University of Wisconsin – Madison, where he received his BA in Political Science and a graduate certificate in GIS. He is currently a Programmer Analyst for the UW-Madison Department of Geoscience working on data visualization, database, and web application development. When not sitting behind a computer, he enjoys rock climbing, cycling, hiking, traveling, cartography, languages, and nearly anything technology related.

Christian S. Perone is an experienced Pythonista, open source collaborator, and the project leader of Pyevolve, a very popular evolutionary computation framework chosen to be part of OpenMDAO, which is an effort by the NASA Glenn Research Center. He has been a programmer for 12 years, using a variety of languages including C, C++, Java, and Python. He has contributed to many open source projects and loves web scraping, open data, web development, machine learning, and evolutionary computation. Currently, he lives in Porto Alegre, Brazil.

Zhang Xiang is an engineer working for the Sina Corporation.

> I'd like to thank my girlfriend, who supports me all the time

www.PacktPub.com

Support files, eBooks, discount offers and more

You might want to visit `www.PacktPub.com` for support files and downloads related to your book.

Did you know that Packt offers eBook versions of every book published, with PDF and ePub files available? You can upgrade to the eBook version at `www.PacktPub.com` and as a print book customer, you are entitled to a discount on the eBook copy. Get in touch with us at `service@packtpub.com` for more details.

At `www.PacktPub.com`, you can also read a collection of free technical articles, sign up for a range of free newsletters and receive exclusive discounts and offers on Packt books and eBooks.

![PACKTLib]

`http://PacktLib.PacktPub.com`

Do you need instant solutions to your IT questions? PacktLib is Packt's online digital book library. Here, you can access, read and search across Packt's entire library of books.

Why Subscribe?

- Fully searchable across every book published by Packt
- Copy and paste, print and bookmark content
- On demand and accessible via web browser

Free Access for Packt account holders

If you have an account with Packt at `www.PacktPub.com`, you can use this to access PacktLib today and view nine entirely free books. Simply use your login credentials for immediate access.

Table of Contents

Preface	**1**
Chapter 1: Installing Beautiful Soup	**7**
Installing Beautiful Soup	**7**
Installing Beautiful Soup in Linux	7
Installing Beautiful Soup using package manager	8
Installing Beautiful Soup using pip or easy_install	9
Installing Beautiful Soup using pip	9
Installing Beautiful Soup using easy_install	9
Installing Beautiful Soup in Windows	10
Verifying Python path in Windows	10
Installing Beautiful Soup using setup.py	12
Using Beautiful Soup without installation	**12**
Verifying the installation	**13**
Quick reference	**13**
Summary	**14**
Chapter 2: Creating a BeautifulSoup Object	**15**
Creating a BeautifulSoup object	**15**
Creating a BeautifulSoup object from a string	16
Creating a BeautifulSoup object from a file-like object	16
Creating a BeautifulSoup object for XML parsing	18
Understanding the features argument	19
Tag	**22**
Accessing the Tag object from BeautifulSoup	22
Name of the Tag object	23
Attributes of a Tag object	23
The NavigableString object	**24**
Quick reference	**24**
Summary	**25**

Table of Contents

Chapter 3: Search Using Beautiful Soup — 27
Searching in Beautiful Soup — 27
Searching with find() — 28
- Finding the first producer — 29
- Explaining find() — 30
Searching with find_all() — 37
- Finding all tertiary consumers — 37
- Understanding parameters used with find_all() — 38
Searching for Tags in relation — 40
- Searching for the parent tags — 40
- Searching for siblings — 42
- Searching for next — 44
- Searching for previous — 45
Using search methods to scrape information from a web page — 46
Quick reference — 51
Summary — 52

Chapter 4: Navigation Using Beautiful Soup — 53
Navigation using Beautiful Soup — 53
Navigating down — 55
- Using the name of the child tag — 55
- Using predefined attributes — 56
- Special attributes for navigating down — 59
Navigating up — 60
- The .parent attribute — 60
- The .parents attribute — 61
Navigating sideways to the siblings — 61
- The .next_sibling attribute — 62
- The .previous_sibling attribute — 62
Navigating to the previous and next objects parsed — 63
Quick reference — 63
Summary — 64

Chapter 5: Modifying Content Using Beautiful Soup — 65
Modifying Tag using Beautiful Soup — 65
Modifying the name property of Tag — 66
Modifying the attribute values of Tag — 68
- Updating the existing attribute value of Tag — 68
- Adding new attribute values to Tag — 69
Deleting the tag attributes — 70
Adding a new tag — 71
Modifying string contents — 73
Using .string to modify the string content — 74
Adding strings using .append(), insert(), and new_string() — 75

Deleting tags from the HTML document	**77**
Deleting the producer using decompose()	77
Deleting the producer using extract()	78
Deleting the contents of a tag using Beautiful Soup	79
Special functions to modify content	**80**
Quick reference	**84**
Summary	**86**
Chapter 6: Encoding Support in Beautiful Soup	**87**
Encoding in Beautiful Soup	**88**
Understanding the original encoding of the HTML document	89
Specifying the encoding of the HTML document	89
Output encoding	**90**
Quick reference	**92**
Summary	**92**
Chapter 7: Output in Beautiful Soup	**93**
Formatted printing	**93**
Unformatted printing	**94**
Output formatters in Beautiful Soup	**95**
The minimal formatter	98
The html formatter	98
The None formatter	99
The function formatter	99
Using get_text()	**100**
Quick reference	**101**
Summary	**102**
Chapter 8: Creating a Web Scraper	**103**
Getting book details from PacktPub.com	**103**
Finding pages with a list of books	104
Finding book details	107
Getting selling prices from Amazon	**109**
Getting the selling price from Barnes and Noble	**111**
Summary	**112**
Index	**113**

Preface

Web scraping is now widely used to get data from websites. Whether it be e-mails, contact information, or selling prices of items, we rely on web scraping techniques as they allow us to collect large data with minimal effort, and also, we don't require database or other backend access to get this data as they are represented as web pages.

Beautiful Soup allows us to get data from HTML and XML pages. This book helps us by explaining the installation and creation of a sample website scraper using Beautiful Soup. Searching and navigation methods are explained with the help of simple examples, screenshots, and code samples in this book. The different parser support offered by Beautiful Soup, supports for scraping pages with encodings, formatting the output, and other tasks related to scraping a page are all explained in detail. Apart from these, practical approaches to understanding patterns on a page, using the developer tools in browsers will enable you to write similar scrapers for any other website.

Also, the practical approach followed in this book will help you to design a simple web scraper to scrape and compare the selling prices of various books from three websites, namely, Amazon, Barnes and Noble, and PacktPub.

What this book covers

Chapter 1, *Installing Beautiful Soup*, covers installing Beautiful Soup 4 on Windows, Linux, and Mac OS, and verifying the installation.

Chapter 2, *Creating a BeautifulSoup Object*, describes creating a `BeautifulSoup` object from a string, file, and web page; discusses different objects such as `Tag`, `NavigableString`, and parser support; and specifies parsers that scrape XML too.

Chapter 3, *Search Using Beautiful Soup*, discusses in detail the different search methods in Beautiful Soup, namely, `find()`, `find_all()`, `find_next()`, and `find_parents()`; code examples for a scraper using search methods to get information from a website; and understanding the application of search methods in combination.

Chapter 4, *Navigation Using Beautiful Soup*, discusses in detail the different navigation methods provided by Beautiful Soup, methods specific to navigating downwards and upwards, and sideways, to the previous and next elements of the HTML tree.

Chapter 5, *Modifying Content Using Beautiful Soup*, discusses modifying the HTML tree using Beautiful Soup, and the creation and deletion of HTML tags. Altering the HTML tag attributes is also covered with the help of simple examples.

Chapter 6, *Encoding Support in Beautiful Soup*, discusses the encoding support in Beautiful Soup, creating a `BeautifulSoup` object for a page with specific encoding, and the encoding supports for output.

Chapter 7, *Output in Beautiful Soup*, discusses formatted and unformatted printing support in Beautiful Soup, specifications of different formatters to format the output, and getting just text from an HTML page.

Chapter 8, *Creating a Web Scraper*, discusses creating a web scraper for three websites, namely, Amazon, Barnes and Noble, and PacktPub, to get the book selling price based on ISBN. Searching and navigation methods used to create the parser, use of developer tools so as to identify the patterns required to create the parser, and the full code sample for scraping the mentioned websites are also explained in this chapter.

What you need for this book

You will need Python Version 2.7.5 or higher and Beautiful Soup Version 4 for this book.

For *Chapter 3*, *Search Using Beautiful Soup* and *Chapter 8*, *Creating a Web Scraper*, you must have an Internet connection to scrape different websites using the code examples provided.

Who this book is for

This book is for beginners in web scraping using Beautiful Soup. Knowing the basics of Python programming (such as functions, variables, and values), and the basics of HTML, and CSS, is important to follow all of the steps in this book. Even though it is not mandatory, knowledge of using developer tools in browsers such as Google Chrome and Firefox will be an advantage when learning the scraper examples in chapters 3 and 8.

Conventions

In this book, you will find a number of styles of text that distinguish between different kinds of information. Here are some examples of these styles, and an explanation of their meaning.

Code words in text, database table names, folder names, filenames, file extensions, pathnames, dummy URLs, user input, and Twitter handles are shown as follows: "The `prettify()` method can be called either on a Beautiful Soup object or any of the `Tag` objects."

A block of code is set as follows:

```
html_markup = """<html>
  <body>&    &amp;   ampersand
    ¢    &cent;   cent
    ©    &copy;   copyright
    ÷    &divide; divide
    >    &gt;     greater than
  </body>
</html>
"""
soup = BeautifulSoup(html_markup,"lxml")
print(soup.prettify())
```

When we wish to draw your attention to a particular part of a code block, the relevant lines or items are set in bold:

UserWarning: "http://www.packtpub.com/books" looks like a URL. Beautiful Soup is not an HTTP client. You should probably use an HTTP client to get the document behind the URL, and feed that document to Beautiful Soup

Any command-line input or output is written as follows:

```
sudo easy_install beautifulsoup4
```

New terms and **important words** are shown in bold. Words that you see on the screen, in menus or dialog boxes for example, appear in the text like this: "The output methods in Beautiful Soup escape only the HTML entities of >,<, and & as >, <, and &amp."

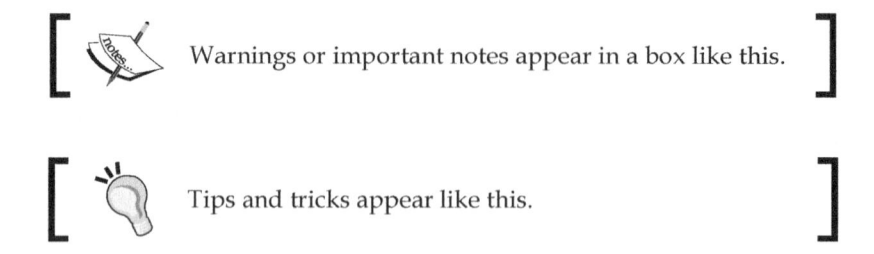

> Warnings or important notes appear in a box like this.

> Tips and tricks appear like this.

Reader feedback

Feedback from our readers is always welcome. Let us know what you think about this book—what you liked or may have disliked. Reader feedback is important for us to develop titles that you really get the most out of.

To send us general feedback, simply send an e-mail to feedback@packtpub.com, and mention the book title via the subject of your message.

If there is a topic that you have expertise in and you are interested in either writing or contributing to a book, see our author guide on www.packtpub.com/authors.

Customer support

Now that you are the proud owner of a Packt book, we have a number of things to help you to get the most from your purchase.

Downloading the example code

You can download the example code files for all Packt books you have purchased from your account at http://www.packtpub.com. If you purchased this book elsewhere, you can visit http://www.packtpub.com/support and register to have the files e-mailed directly to you.

Errata

Although we have taken every care to ensure the accuracy of our content, mistakes do happen. If you find a mistake in one of our books—maybe a mistake in the text or the code—we would be grateful if you would report this to us. By doing so, you can save other readers from frustration and help us improve subsequent versions of this book. If you find any errata, please report them by visiting http://www.packtpub.com/submit-errata, selecting your book, clicking on the **errata submission form** link, and entering the details of your errata. Once your errata are verified, your submission will be accepted and the errata will be uploaded on our website, or added to any list of existing errata, under the Errata section of that title. Any existing errata can be viewed by selecting your title from http://www.packtpub.com/support.

Piracy

Piracy of copyright material on the Internet is an ongoing problem across all media. At Packt, we take the protection of our copyright and licenses very seriously. If you come across any illegal copies of our works, in any form, on the Internet, please provide us with the location address or website name immediately so that we can pursue a remedy.

Please contact us at copyright@packtpub.com with a link to the suspected pirated material.

We appreciate your help in protecting our authors, and our ability to bring you valuable content.

Questions

You can contact us at questions@packtpub.com if you are having a problem with any aspect of the book, and we will do our best to address it.

1
Installing Beautiful Soup

Before we begin using Beautiful Soup, we should ensure that it is properly installed on our machine. The steps required are so simple that any user can install this in no time. In this chapter, we will be covering the following topics:

- Installing Beautiful Soup
- Verifying the installation of Beautiful Soup

Installing Beautiful Soup

Python supports the installation of third-party modules such as Beautiful Soup. In the best case scenario, we can expect that the module developer might have prepared a platform-specific installer, for example, an executable installer, in the case of Windows; an rpm package, in the case of Red Hat-based Linux operating systems (Red Hat, Open Suse, and so on); and a Debian package, in the case of Debian-based operating systems (Debian, Ubuntu, and so on). But this is not always the case and we should know the alternatives if the platform-specific installer is not available. We will discuss the different installation options available for Beautiful Soup in different operating systems, such as Linux, Windows, and Mac OS X. The Python version that we are going to use in the later examples for installing Beautiful Soup is Python 2.7.5 and the instructions for Python 3 are probably different. You can directly go to the installation section corresponding to the operating system.

Installing Beautiful Soup in Linux

Installing Beautiful Soup is pretty simple and straightforward in Linux machines. For recent versions of Debian or Ubuntu, Beautiful Soup is available as a package and we can install this using the system package manager. For other versions of Debian or Ubuntu, where Beautiful Soup is not available as a package, we can use alternative methods for installation.

Installing Beautiful Soup

Normally, these are the following three ways to install Beautiful Soup in Linux machines:

- Using package manager
- Using `pip`
- Using `easy_install`

The choices are ranked depending on the complexity levels and to avoid the trial-and-error method. The easiest method is always using the package manager since it requires less effort from the user, so we will cover this first. If the installation is successful in one step, we don't need to do the next because the three steps mentioned previously do the same thing.

Installing Beautiful Soup using package manager

Linux machines normally come with a package manager to install various packages. In the recent version of Debian or Ubuntu, since Beautiful Soup is available as a package, we will be using the system package manager for installation. In Linux machines such as Ubuntu and Debian, the default package manager is based on `apt-get` and hence we will use `apt-get` to do the task.

Just open up a terminal and type in the following command:

```
sudo apt-get install python-bs4
```

The preceding command will install Beautiful Soup Version 4 in our Linux operating system. Installing new packages in the system normally requires root user privileges, which is why we append `sudo` in front of the `apt-get` command. If we didn't append `sudo`, we will basically end up with a permission denied error. If the packages are already updated, we will see the following success message in the command line itself:

```
vineeth@vineeth-kochicoders:~$ sudo apt-get install python-bs4
Reading package lists... Done
Building dependency tree
Reading state information... Done
The following NEW packages will be installed:
  python-bs4
0 upgraded, 1 newly installed, 0 to remove and 228 not upgraded.
Need to get 0 B/62.9 kB of archives.
After this operation, 327 kB of additional disk space will be used.
Selecting previously unselected package python-bs4.
(Reading database ... 155233 files and directories currently installed.)
Unpacking python-bs4 (from .../python-bs4_4.1.2-1_all.deb) ...
Setting up python-bs4 (4.1.2-1) ...
vineeth@vineeth-kochicoders:~$
```

Since we are using a recent version of Ubuntu or Debian, `python-bs4` will be listed in the `apt` repository. But if the preceding command fails with `Package Not Found Error`, it means that the package list is not up-to-date. This normally happens if we have just installed our operating system and the package list is not downloaded from the package repository. In this case, we need to first update the package list using the following command:

```
sudo apt-get update
```

The preceding command will update the necessary package list from the online package repositories. After this, we need to try the preceding command to install Beautiful Soup.

In the older versions of the Linux operating system, even after running the `apt-get update` command, we might not be able to install Beautiful Soup because it might not be available in the repositories. In these scenarios, we can rely on the other methods of installation using either `pip` or `easy_install`.

Installing Beautiful Soup using pip or easy_install

The `pip` and `easy_install` are the tools used for managing and installing Python packages. Either of them can be used to install Beautiful Soup.

Installing Beautiful Soup using pip

From the terminal, type the following command:

```
sudo pip install beautifulsoup4
```

The preceding command will install Beautiful Soup Version 4 in the system after downloading the necessary packages from `http://pypi.python.org/`.

Installing Beautiful Soup using easy_install

The `easy_install` tool installs the package from **Python Package Index** (**PyPI**). So, in the terminal, type the following command:

```
sudo easy_install beautifulsoup4
```

All the previous methods to install Beautiful Soup in Linux will not work if you do not have an active network connection. So, in case everything fails, we can still install Beautiful Soup. The last option would be to use the `setup.py` script that comes with every Python package downloaded from `pypi.python.org`. This method is also the recommended method to install Beautiful Soup in Windows and in Mac OS X machines. So, we will discuss this method in the *Installing Beautiful Soup in Windows* section.

Installing Beautiful Soup in Windows

In Windows, we will make use of the recent Python package for Beautiful Soup available from `https://pypi.python.org/packages/source/b/beautifulsoup4/` and use the `setup.py` script to install Beautiful Soup. But before doing this, it will be easier for us if we add the path of Python in the system path. The next section discusses setting up the path to Python on a Windows machine.

Verifying Python path in Windows

Often, the path to `python.exe` will not be added to an environment variable by default in Windows. So, in order to check this from the Windows command-line prompt, you need to type the following command:

`python.`

The preceding command will work without any errors if the path to Python is already added in the environment path variable or we are already within the Python installed directory. But, it would be good to check the path variable for the Python directory entry.

If it doesn't exist in the path variable, we have to find out the actual path, which is entirely dependent on where you installed Python. For Python 2.x, it will be by `C:\Python2x` by default, and for Python 3.x, the path will be `C:\Python3x` by default.

We have to add this to the `Path` environment variable in the Windows machine. For this, right-click on **My Computer** | **Properties** | **Environment Variables** | **System Variable**.

Pick the `Path` variable and add the following section to the `Path` variable:

`;C:\PythonXY for example C:\Python27`

Chapter 1

This is shown in the following screenshot:

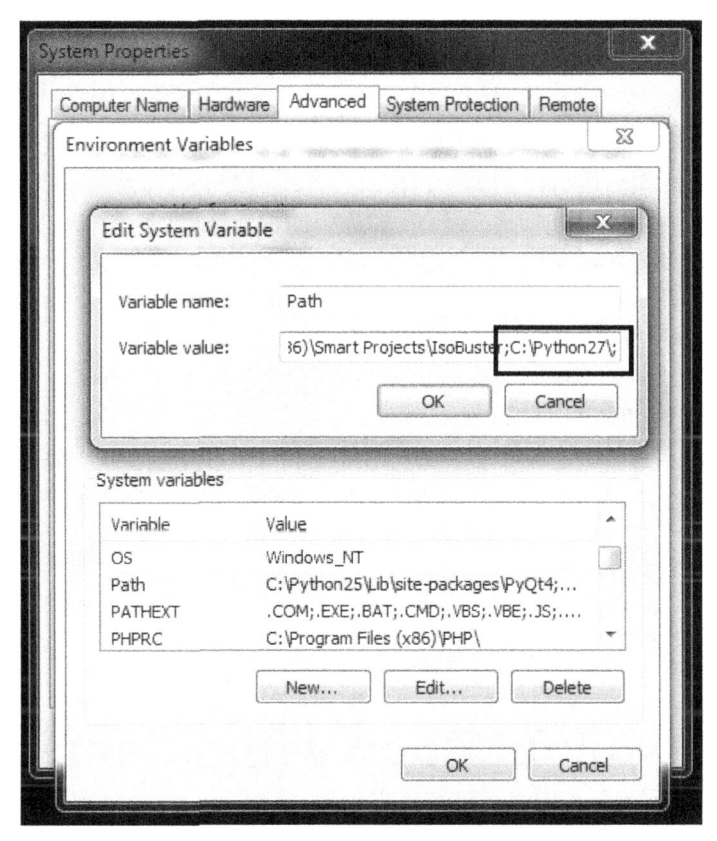

Adding Python path in Windows (Python 2.7 is used in this example)

After the Python path is ready, we can follow the steps for installing Beautiful Soup on a Windows machine.

> The method, which will be explained in the next section, of installing Beautiful Soup using `setup.py` is the same for Linux, Windows, and Mac OS X operating systems.

Installing Beautiful Soup using setup.py

We can install Python packages using the setup.py script that comes with every Python package downloaded from the Python package index website: https://pypi.python.org/. The following steps are used to install the Beautiful Soup using setup.py:

1. Download the latest tarball from https://pypi.python.org/packages/source/b/beautifulsoup4/.
2. Unzip it to a folder (for example, BeautifulSoup).
3. Open up the command-line prompt and navigate to the folder where you have unzipped the folder as follows:

   cd BeautifulSoup

   python setup.py install.

4. The python setup.py install line will install Beautiful Soup in our system.

> We are not done with the list of possible options to use Beautiful Soup. We can use Beautiful Soup in our applications even if all of the options outlined until now fail.

Using Beautiful Soup without installation

The installation processes that we have discussed till now normally copy the module contents to a chosen installation directory. This varies from operating system to operating system and the path is normally /usr/local/lib/pythonX.Y/site-packages in Linux operating systems such as Debian and C:\PythonXY\Lib\site-packages in Windows (where X and Y represent the corresponding versions, such as Python 2.7). When we use import statements in the Python interpreter or as a part of a Python script, normally what the Python interpreter does is look in the predefined Python Path variable and look for the module in those directories. So, installing actually means copying the module contents into the predefined directory or copying this to some other location and adding the location into the Python path. The following method of using Beautiful Soup without going through the installation can be used in any operating system, such as Windows, Linux, or Mac OS X:

1. Download the latest version of Beautiful Soup package from https://pypi.python.org/packages/source/b/beautifulsoup4/.
2. Unzip the package.
3. Copy the bs4 directory into the directory where we want to place all our Python Beautiful Soup scripts.

After we perform all the preceding steps, we are good to use Beautiful Soup. In order to import Beautiful Soup in this case, either we need to open the terminal in the directory where the `bs4` directory exists or add this directory to the Python `Path` variable; otherwise, we will get the `module not found` error. This extra step is required because the method is specific to a project where the `bs4` directory is included. But in the case of installing methods, as we have seen previously, Beautiful Soup will be available globally and can be used in any of the projects, and so the additional steps are not required.

Verifying the installation

To verify the installation, perform the following steps:

1. Open up the Python interpreter in a terminal by using the following command:

   `python`

2. Now, we can issue a simple import statement to see whether we have successfully installed Beautiful Soup or not by using the following command:

   `from bs4 import BeautifulSoup`

If we did not install Beautiful Soup and instead copied the `bs4` directory in the workspace, we have to change to the directory where we have placed the `bs4` directory before using the preceding commands.

Quick reference

The following table is an overview of commands and their implications:

`sudo apt-get install python-bs4`	This command is used for installing Python using a package manger in Linux.
`sudo pip install beautifulsoup4`	This command is used for installing Python using `pip`.
`sudo easy_install beautifulsoup4`	This command is used for installing Python using `easy install`.
`python setup.py install`	This command is used for installing Python using `setup.py`.
`from bs4 import BeautifulSoup`	This command is used for verifying installation.

Summary

In this chapter, we covered the various options to install Beautiful Soup in Linux machines. We also discussed a way of installing Beautiful Soup in Windows, Linux, and Mac OS X using the Python `setup.py` script itself. We also discussed the method to use Beautiful Soup without even installing it. The verification of the Beautiful Soup installation was also covered.

In the next chapter, we are going to have a first look at Beautiful Soup by learning the different methods of converting HTML/XML content to different Beautiful Soup objects and thereby understanding the properties of Beautiful Soup.

2
Creating a BeautifulSoup Object

We saw how to install Beautiful Soup in Linux, Windows, and Mac OS X machines in *Chapter 1, Installing Beautiful Soup*.

Beautiful Soup is widely used for getting data from web pages. We can use Beautiful Soup to extract any data in an HTML/XML document, for example, to get all links in a page or to get text inside tags on the page. In order to achieve this, Beautiful Soup offers us different objects, and simple searching and navigation methods.

Any input HTML/XML document is converted to different Beautiful Soup objects, and based on the different properties and methods of these objects, we can extract the required data. The list of objects in Beautiful Soup includes the following:

- `BeautifulSoup`
- `Tag`
- `NavigableString`

Creating a BeautifulSoup object

Creating a `BeautifulSoup` object is the starting point of any Beautiful Soup project. A `BeautifulSoup` object represents the input HTML/XML document used for its creation.

`BeautifulSoup` is created by passing a string or a file-like object (this can be an open handle to the files stored locally in our machine or a web page).

Creating a BeautifulSoup object from a string

A string can be passed to the BeautifulSoup constructor to create an object as follows:

```
helloworld = "<p>Hello World</p>"
soup_string = BeautifulSoup(helloworld)
```

> **Downloading the example code**
> You can download the example code files for all Packt books you have purchased from your account at http://www.packtpub.com. If you purchased this book elsewhere, you can visit http://www.packtpub.com/support and register to have the files e-mailed directly to you.

The previous code will create the BeautifulSoup object based on the input string helloworld. We can see that the input has been treated as HTML and the content of the object can be verified by print(soup_string).

```
<html><body><p>Helloworld</p></body></html>
```

> The output of the previous code can be different in some systems based on the parser used. This is explained later in this chapter.

During the creation of the object, Beautiful Soup converts the input markup (HTML/XML) to a tree structure using the supported parsers. While doing so, the markup will be represented as different Beautiful Soup objects such as BeautifulSoup, Tag, and NavigableString.

Creating a BeautifulSoup object from a file-like object

A file-like object can also be passed to the BeautifulSoup constructor to create the object. This is useful in parsing an online web page, which is the most common use of Beautiful Soup.

For example, consider the case where we need to get a list of all the books published by Packt Publishing, which is available at http://www.packtpub.com/books. In order to reduce the overhead of visiting this URL from our browser to get the page content as String, it is appropriate to create the BeautifulSoup object by providing the file-like object of the URL.

```
import urllib2
from bs4 import BeautifulSoup
```

```
url = "http://www.packtpub.com/books"
page = urllib2.urlopen(url)
soup_packtpage = BeautifulSoup(page)
```

In the previous Python script, we have used the `urllib2` module, which is a native Python module, to open the http://www.packtpub.com/books page. The `urllib2.urlopen()` method returns a file-like object for the input URL. Then we create the `BeautifulSoup` object, `soup_packtpage`, by passing the file-like object.

> Creating a `BeautifulSoup` object using a URL file-like object is the efficient way to deal with online web pages.

We learned how to create a `BeautifulSoup` object by passing a file-like object for a URL in the previous example. Similarly, we can pass the file object for a local file to the `BeautifulSoup` constructor.

For this, create a local folder in your machine by executing the command `mkdir Soup` from a terminal. Create an HTML file, `foo.html`, in this folder using `touch Soup/foo.html`. From the same terminal, change to the directory just created using `cd Soup`.

Now let us see the creation of `BeautifulSoup` using the file `foo.html`.

```
with open("foo.html","r") as foo_file:
    soup_foo = BeautifulSoup(foo_file)
```

The previous lines of code create a `BeautifulSoup` object based on the contents of the local file, `foo.html`.

Beautiful Soup has a basic warning mechanism to notify whether we have passed a filename instead of the file object.

Let us look at the next code line:

```
soup_foo = BeautifulSoup("foo.html")
```

This will produce the following warning:

`UserWarning: "foo.html" looks like a filename, not markup. You should probably open this file and pass the filehandle into Beautiful Soup.`

But still a `BeautifulSoup` object is created assuming the string (`"foo.html"`) that we passed as HTML.

Creating a BeautifulSoup Object

The `print(soup_foo)` code line will give the following output:

```
<html><body><p>foo.html</p></body></html>
```

The same warning mechanism also notifies us if we tried to pass in a URL instead of the URL file object.

```
soup_url = BeautifulSoup("http://www.packtpub.com/books")
```

The previous line of code will produce the following warning:

UserWarning: "http://www.packtpub.com/books" looks like a URL. Beautiful Soup is not an HTTP client. You should probably use an HTTP client to get the document behind the URL, and feed that document to Beautiful Soup

Here also the `BeautifulSoup` object is created by considering the string (URL) as HTML.

```
print(soup_url)
```

The previous code will give the following output:

```
<html><body><p>http://www.packtpub.com/books</p></body></html>
```

So we should pass either the file handle or string to the `BeautifulSoup` constructor.

Creating a BeautifulSoup object for XML parsing

Beautiful Soup can also be used for XML parsing. While creating a `BeautifulSoup` object, the `TreeBuilder` class is selected by Beautiful Soup for the creation of HTML/XML tree. The `TreeBuilder` class is used for creating the HTML/XML tree from the input document. The default behavior is to select any of the HTML `TreeBuilder` objects, which use the default HTML parser, leading to the creation of the HTML tree. In the previous example, using the string `helloworld`, we can verify the content of the `soup_string` object, which shows that the input is treated as HTML by default.

```
soup_string = BeautifulSoup(helloworld)
print(soup_string)
```

The output for the previous code snippet is as follows:

```
<html><body><p>Hello World</p></body></html>
```

If we want Beautiful Soup to consider the input to be parsed as XML instead, we need to explicitly specify this using the `features` argument in the `BeautifulSoup` constructor. By specifying the `features` argument, `BeautifulSoup` will be able to pick up the best suitable `TreeBuilder` that satisfies the features we requested.

Understanding the features argument

The `TreeBuilders` class use an underlying parser for input processing. Each `TreeBuilder` will have a different set of features based on the parser it uses. So the input is treated differently based on the features argument being passed to the constructor. The parsers currently used by different `TreeBuilders` in Beautiful Soup are as follows:

- `lxml`
- `html5lib`
- `html.parser`

The `features` argument of the `BeautifulSoup` constructor can accept either a list of strings or a string value. The currently supported features by each `TreeBuilder` and the underlying parsers are described in the following table:

Features	TreeBuilder	Parser
['lxml','html','fast','permissive']	LXMLTreeBuilder	lxml
['html','html5lib','permissive','strict','html5']	HTML5TreeBuilder	html5lib
['html','strict','html.parser']	HTMLParserTreeBuilder	html.parser
['xml','lxml','permissive','fast']	LXMLTreeBuilderForXML	lxml

The `features` argument can be specified as a list of strings or a string value. Beautiful Soup picks the best suitable `TreeBuilder`, which has the feature(s) specified. The order of picking a `Treebuilder` in the case of an HTML document is based on the priority of the parsers upon which they are built. The first being `lxml`, followed by `html5lib`, and at last `html.parser`. For example, if we provide `html` as the feature, Beautiful Soup will pick `lXmlTreeBuilder`, if the `lxml` parser is available. If the `lxml` parser is not available, it picks `HTML5TreeBuilder` based on the `html5lib` parser, and if the `html5lib` parser is also not available, then `HTMLPraserTreeBuilder` is picked based on the `html.parser`. For XML, since `lxml` is the only available parser, `LXMLTreeBuilderForXML` is always selected.

Creating a BeautifulSoup Object

We can specify the `features` argument in the `BeautifulSoup` constructor for considering the input for XML processing as follows:

```
soup_xml = BeautifulSoup(helloworld,features= "xml")
```

Another alternative is by using the following code line:

```
soup_xml = BeautifulSoup(helloworld, "xml")
```

In the previous code, we passed `xml` as the value for the `features` argument and created the `soup_xml` object. We can see that the same content (`"<p>Helloworld</p>"`) is now being treated as XML instead of HTML.

```
print(soup_xml)

#output
<?xml version="1.0" encoding="utf-8"?>
<p>Hello World</p>
```

In the previous example, Beautiful Soup has picked `LXMLTreeBuilderForXML` based on the `lxml` parser and parsed the input as XML.

> The `features` argument helps us to choose between HTML/XML parsing for the document.

By providing the `features` argument we are specifying the features that a `TreeBuilder` should have. In case Beautiful Soup is unable to find a `TreeBuilder` with the given features, an error is thrown. For example, assume that `lxml`, which is the only parser currently used by Beautiful Soup for XML processing, is not present in the system. In this case, if we use the following line of code:

```
soup_xml = BeautifulSoup(helloworld,features= "xml")
```

The previous code will fail and throw the following error (since `lxml` is not installed in the system):

```
bs4.FeatureNotFound: Couldn't find a tree builder with the
  features you requested: xml. Do you need to install a parser
  library?
```

In this case, we should install the required parsers using `easy_install`, `pip`, or `setup.py install`.

It is always a better practice to specify the parser to be used while creating a `BeautifulSoup` object. This is due to the fact that different parsers parse the content differently. This is more evident in cases where we give invalid HTML content to parse. The three parsers discussed previously produce three types of HTML trees in the case of an invalid HTML. For example:

```
invalid_html = '<a invalid content'
```

Here the HTML is invalid since there is no closing `</a>` tag. The processing of this invalid HTML using the previously mentioned parsers is given as follows:

- By using the `lxml` parser, which is shown as follows:

    ```
    soup_invalid_html = BeautifulSoup(invalid_html,'lxml')
    ```

    The `print(soup_invalid_html)` code line will give the HTML tree produced using the `lxml` parser.

    ```
    <html><body><a invalid content=""></a></body></html>
    ```

    From the output, it is clear that the `lxml` parser has processed the invalid HTML. It added the closing `</a>` tag and also considered the invalid content as an attribute of the `<a>` tag. Apart from this, it has also added the `<html>` and `<body>` tags, which was not present in the input. Addition of the `<html>` and `<body>` tags will be done by default if we use `lxml`.

- By using the `html5lib` parser, which is shown as follows:

    ```
    soup_invalid_html = BeautifulSoup(invalid_html,'html5lib')
    ```

    The `print(soup_invalid_html)` code line will show us the HTML tree produced using the `html5lib` parser.

    ```
    <html><head></head><body></body></html>
    ```

    From the output, it is clear that the `html5lib` parser has added the `<html>`, `<head>`, and `<body>` tags, which was not present in the input. For example, the `lxml` parser and the `html5lib` parser will also add these tags for any input. But at the same time, it has discarded the invalid `<a>` tag to produce a different representation of the input.

- By using the `html.parser`, which is shown as follows:

    ```
    soup_invalid_html =
       BeautifulSoup(invalid_html,'html.parser')
    ```

Creating a BeautifulSoup Object

The `print(soup_invalid_html)` code line will show us the HTML tree produced using the `html.parser`.

The `html.parser` has discarded the invalid HTML and produced an empty tree. Unlike the other parsers, it doesn't add any of the `<html>`, `<head>`, or `<body>` tags.

So, it is good to specify the parser by giving the `features` argument because this helps to ensure that the input is processed in the same manner across different machines. Otherwise, there is a possibility that the same code will break in one of the machines if some invalid HTML is present, as the default parser that is picked up by Beautiful Soup will produce a different tree. Specifying the `features` argument helps to ensure that the tree generated is identical across all machines.

While creating the `BeautifulSoup` object, other objects are also created, which include the following:

- Tag
- NavigableString

Tag

The `Tag` object represents different tags of HTML and XML documents. The creation of `Tag` objects is done when parsing the documents. The different HTML/XML tags identified during parsing are represented as corresponding `Tag` objects and these objects will have attributes and contents of the HTML/XML tag. The `Tag` objects can be used for searching and navigation within the HTML/XML document.

Accessing the Tag object from BeautifulSoup

`BeautifulSoup` allows us to access any `Tag` object. For example, we can access the first occurrence of the `<a>` tag in the next example by simply calling the name of the tag `<a>`.

```
html_atag = """<html><body><p>Test html a tag example</p>
<a href="http://www.packtpub.com'>Home</a>
<a href="http;//www.packtpub.com/books'>Books</a>
</body>
</html>"""
soup  = BeautifulSoup(html_atag,'lxml')
atag = soup.a
print(atag)
```

[22]

The previous script will print the first `<a>` tag in the document. We can see that `type(atag)` is `'bs4.element.Tag'`.

HTML/XML tags have names (for example, the name for the tag `<a>` is a and the tag `<p>` is p) and attributes (for example, class, id, and style). The `Tag` object allows us to get the name and attributes associated with each HTML tag.

Name of the Tag object

The name of the `Tag` object is accessible via the `.name` property.

```
tagname = atag.name
print tagname
```

The previous code prints the name of the object `atag`, which is nothing but the name of the tag `<a>`.

We can change the name of the tag by changing the value of the `.name` property.

This is shown in the following example:

```
atag.name = 'p'
print(soup)

#output
<html><body><p>Test html a tag example</p>
  <p href="http://www.packtpub.com'>Home</p>
  <a href="http://www.packtpub.com/books'>Books</a>
</body></html>
```

From the output, we can see that first the `<a>` tag was replaced with the `<p>` tag.

Attributes of a Tag object

Attributes give a tag meaning and context. In the previous example, the `href` attribute adds the URL information for the `<a>` tag. In HTML pages, the tags might have different attributes, for example, class, id, and style. The attributes of a tag can be accessed by considering the `Tag` object as a dictionary.

```
atag = soup_atag.a
print (atag['href'] )

#output
http://www.packtpub.com
```

[23]

Creating a BeautifulSoup Object

The previous code prints the URL (`http://www.packtpub.com`) associated with the first `<a>` tag by accessing the value of the `href` attribute.

Different attributes associated with a tag can be accessed using the `.attrs` property.

The `print(atag.attrs)` code line gives `{'href':' http://www.packtpub.com'}`.

Apart from the name and attributes, a `Tag` object has helper methods for navigating and searching through the document, which we will discuss in the following chapters.

The NavigableString object

A `NavigableString` object holds the text within an HTML or an XML tag. This is a Python Unicode string with methods for searching and navigation. Sometimes we may need to navigate to other tags or text within an HTML/XML document based on the current text. With a normal Python Unicode string, the searching and navigation methods will not work. The `NavigableString` object will give us the text within a tag as a Unicode string, together with the different methods for searching and navigating the tree.

We can get the text stored inside a particular tag by using `".string"`.

```
first_a_string = soup_atag.string
```

In the previous code, the `NavigableString` object (`first_a_string`) is created and this holds the string inside the first `<a>` tag, `u'Home'`.

Quick reference

You can view the following references to get an overview of creating the following objects:

- BeautifulSoup
    - `soup = BeautifulSoup(string)`
    - `soup = BeautifulSoup(string,features="xml")   #for xml`
- Tag
    - `tag = soup.tag #accessing a tag`
    - `tag.name     #Tag name`
    - `tag['attribute']  #Tag attribute`

3
Search Using Beautiful Soup

We saw the creation of the BeautifulSoup object and other objects, such as Tag and NavigableString in *Chapter 2, Creating a BeautifulSoup Object*. The HTML/XML document is converted to these objects for the ease of searching and navigating within the document.

In this chapter, we will learn the different searching methods provided by Beautiful Soup to search based on tag name, attribute values of tag, text within the document, regular expression, and so on. At the end, we will make use of these searching methods to scrape data from an online web page.

Searching in Beautiful Soup

Beautiful Soup helps in scraping information from web pages. Useful information is scattered across web pages as text or attribute values of different tags. In order to scrape such pages, it is necessary to search through the entire page for different tags based on the attribute values or tag name or texts within the document. To facilitate this, Beautiful Soup comes with inbuilt search methods listed as follows:

- `find()`
- `find_all()`
- `find_parent()`
- `find_parents()`
- `find_next_sibling()`
- `find_next_siblings()`
- `find_previous_sibling()`
- `find_previous_siblings()`

- `find_previous()`
- `find_all_previous()`
- `find_next()`
- `find_all_next()`

Searching with find()

In this chapter, we will use the following HTML code for explaining the search using Beautiful Soup. We can save this as an HTML file named `ecologicalpyramid.html` inside the `Soup` directory we created in the previous chapter.

```html
<html>
  <body>
  <div class="ecopyramid">
    <ul id="producers">
      <li class="producerlist">
        <div class="name">plants</div>
        <div class="number">100000</div>
      </li>
      <li class="producerlist">
        <div class="name">algae</div>
        <div class="number">100000</div>
      </li>
    </ul>
    <ul id="primaryconsumers">
      <li class="primaryconsumerlist">
        <div class="name">deer</div>
        <div class="number">1000</div>
      </li>
      <li class="primaryconsumerlist">
        <div class="name">rabbit</div>
        <div class="number">2000</div>
      </li>
    </ul>
    <ul id="secondaryconsumers">
      <li class="secondaryconsumerlist">
        <div class="name">fox</div>
        <div class="number">100</div>
      </li>
      <li class="secondaryconsumerlist">
        <div class="name">bear</div>
```

```html
          <div class="number">100</div>
        </li>
      </ul>
      <ul id="tertiaryconsumers">
        <li class="tertiaryconsumerlist">
          <div class="name">lion</div>
          <div class="number">80</div>
        </li>
        <li class="tertiaryconsumerlist">
          <div class="name">tiger</div>
          <div class="number">50</div>
        </li>
      </ul>
    </body>
</html>
```

The preceding HTML is a simple representation of the ecological pyramid. To find the first producer, primary consumer, or secondary consumer, we can use Beautiful Soup search methods. In general, to find the first entry of any tag within a `BeautifulSoup` object, we can use the `find()` method.

Finding the first producer

In the case of the ecological pyramid example of the HTML content, we can easily recognize that the producers are within the first `<ul>` tag. Since the producers come as the first entry for the `<ul>` tag within the whole HTML document, it is easy to find the first producer using the `find()` method. The HTML tree that represents the first producer is shown in the following diagram:

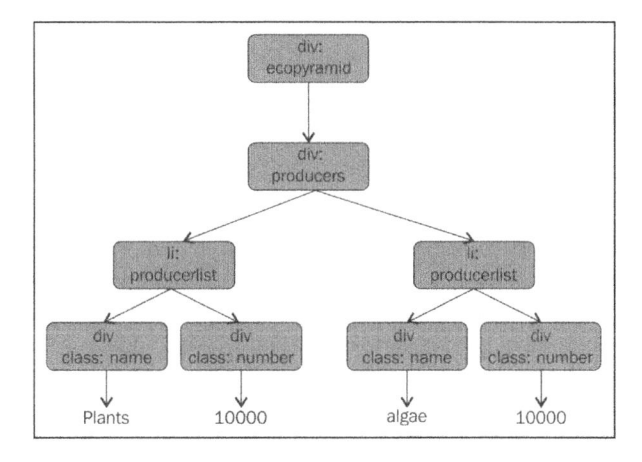

Now, we can change to the `Soup` directory using the following command:

`cd Soup`.

We can save the following code as `ecologicalpyramid.py` and use `python ecologicalpyramid.py` to run it, or we can run the code from Python interpreter. Using the following code, we will create a `BeautifulSoup` object using the `ecologicalpyramid.html` file:

```
from bs4 import BeautifulSoup
with open("ecologicalpyramid.html","r") as ecological_pyramid:
    soup = BeautifulSoup(ecological_pyramid,"lxml")
producer_entries = soup.find("ul")
print(producer_entries.li.div.string)

#output
plants
```

Since producers come as the first entry for the `<ul>` tag, we can use the `find()` method, which normally searches for only the first occurrence of a particular tag in a `BeautifulSoup` object. We store this in `producer_entries`. The next line prints the name of the first producer. From the previous HTML diagram, we can understand that the first producer is stored inside the first `<div>` tag of the first `<li>` tag that immediately follows the first `<ul>` tag, as shown in the following code:

```
<ul id="producers">
  <li class="producerlist">
    <div class="name">plants</div>
    <div class="number">100000</div>
  </li>
</ul>
```

So, after running the preceding code, we will get `plants`, which is the first producer, as the output.

Explaining find()

At this point, we know that `find()` is used to search for the first occurrence of any items within a `BeautifulSoup` object. The signature of the `find()` method is as follows:

`find(name,attrs,recursive,text,**kwargs)`

As the signature implies, the `find()` method accepts the parameters, such as `name`, `attrs`, `recursive`, `text`, and `**kwargs`. Parameters such as `name`, `attrs`, and `text` are the filters that can be applied on a `find()` method.

Different filters can be applied on `find()` for the following cases:

- Searching a tag, which corresponds to filtering based on the `name` parameter
- Searching text, which corresponds to the filtering based on the `text` parameter
- Searching based on a regular expression
- Searching based on attribute values of a tag, which corresponds to the filtering based on the `attrs` parameter
- Searching based on functions

Searching for tags

Finding the first producer was an example of a simple filter that can be done using the `find()` method. We basically passed the `ul` string, which represented the name of the `<ul>` tag to the `find()` method. Likewise, we can pass any tag name to the `find()` method to get its first occurrence. In this case, `find()` returns a Beautiful Soup `Tag` object. For example, refer to the following code:

```
tag_li = soup.find("li")
print(type(tag_li))

#output
<class 'bs4.element.Tag'>
```

The preceding code finds the first occurrence of the `li` tag within the HTML document and then prints the type of `tag_li`.

This can also be achieved by passing the `name` argument as follows:

```
tag_li = soup.find(name="li")
print(type(tag_li))

#output
<class 'bs4.element.Tag'>
```

By default, `find()` returns the first `Tag` object with name equals to the string we passed.

Searching for text

If we pass a string to search using the `find()` method, it will search for tags with the given name by default. But, if we want to search only for text within the `BeautifulSoup` object, we can use it as follows:

```
search_for_stringonly = soup.find(text="fox")

#output
fox
```

The preceding code will search for the occurrence of the `fox` text within the ecological pyramid. Searching for the text using Beautiful Soup is case sensitive. For example, `case_sensitive_string = soup.find(text="Fox")` will return `None`.

Searching based on regular expressions

The `find()` method can search based on a regular expression. This normally comes in handy when we have an HTML page with no pattern like the preceding producer example.

Let us take an example where we are given a page with e-mail IDs, as mentioned in the following code, and we are asked to find the first e-mail ID:

```
<br/>
<div>The below HTML has the information that has email ids.</div>
   abc@example.com
<div>xyz@example.com</div>
<span>foo@example.com</span>
```

Here, the e-mail IDs are scattered across the page with one inside the `<div>` tag, another inside the `<span>` tag, and the first one, which is not enclosed by any tag. It is difficult here to find the first e-mail ID. But if we can represent the e-mail ID using regular expression, `find()` can search based on the expression to get the first e-mail ID.

So in this case, we just need to form the regular expression for the e-mail ID and pass it to the `find()` method. The `find()` method will use the regular expression, the `match()` method, to find a match for the given regular expression.

Let us find the first e-mail ID using the following code:

```
import re
from bs4 import BeautifulSoup
email_id_example = """<br/>
<div>The below HTML has the information that has email ids.</div>
   abc@example.com
```

```
<div>xyz@example.com</div>
<span>foo@example.com</span>
"""
soup = BeautifulSoup(email_id_example,"lxml")
emailid_regexp = re.compile("\w+@\w+\.\w+")
first_email_id = soup.find(text=emailid_regexp)
print(first_email_id)

#output
abc@example.com
```

In the preceding code, we created the regular expression for the e-mail ID in the `emailid_regexp` variable. The pattern we used previously is \w+@\w+\. The \w+ symbol represents one or more alphanumeric characters followed by @, and then again followed by one or more alphanumeric character, then a . symbol, and one or more alphanumeric character. This matches the e-mail ID in the preceding example. We then passed the `emailid_regexp` variable to the `find()` method to find the first text that matches the preceding pattern.

Searching based on attribute values of a tag

We can use `find()` to search based on the attribute values of a tag. In the previous ecological pyramid example, we can see that primary consumers are within the `<ul>` tag with the `primaryconsumers` ID. In this case, it is easy to use `find()` with the argument as the attribute value that we are looking for.

Finding the first primary consumer

Finding the producer was an easy task, since it was the first entry for the `<ul>` tag. But what about the first primary consumer? It is not inside the first `<ul>` tag. By careful analysis, we can see that primary consumers are inside the second `<ul>` tag with the `id="primaryconsumers"` attribute. In this case, we can use Beautiful Soup to search based on the attribute value, assuming we already created the `soup` object. In the following code, we are storing the first occurrence of the tag with the `id ="primaryconsumers"` attribute in `primary_consumers`:

```
primary_consumers = soup.find(id="primaryconsumers")
print(primary_consumers.li.div.string)

#output
deer
```

Search Using Beautiful Soup

If we analyze the HTML, we can see that the first primary consumer is stored as follows:

```
<ul id="primaryconsumers">
  <li class="primaryconsumerlist">
    <div class="name">deer</div>
    <div class="number">1000</div>
  </li>
</ul>
```

We can see that the first primary consumer is stored inside the first `<div>` tag of the first `<li>` tag. The second line prints the string stored inside this `<div>` tag, which is the first primary consumer name, which is `deer`.

Searching based on attribute values will work for most of the attributes, such as `id`, `style`, and `title`. But, there are some exceptions in the case of a couple of attributes as follows:

- Custom attributes
- Class

In these cases, although we can't go directly with the attribute-value-based search, we can use the `attrs` argument that can be passed into the `find()` method.

Searching based on custom attributes

In HTML5, it is possible to add custom attributes such as `data-custom` to a tag. If we want Beautiful Soup to search based on these attributes, it will not be possible to use it like we did in the case of the `id` attribute.

For searching based on the `id` attribute, we used the following code line:

```
soup.find(id="primaryconsumer")
```

But, if we use the attribute value the same way for the following HTML, the code will throw an error as `keyword can't be an expression`:

```
customattr = """'<p data-custom="custom">custom attribute
  example</p>"""
customsoup = BeautifulSoup(customattr,'lxml')
customSoup.find(data-custom="custom")
```

The error is thrown because Python variables cannot contain a - character and the `data-custom` variable that we passed contained a - character.

In such cases, we need to pass in the keyword arguments as a dictionary in the `attrs` argument as follows:

```
using_attrs = customsoup.find(attrs={'data-custom':'custom'})
print(using_attrs)

#output
'<p data-custom="custom">custom attribute example</p>'
```

Searching based on the CSS class

The `class` argument is a reserved keyword in Python and so, we will not be able to use the keyword argument `class`. So in the case of the CSS classes also, we can use the same process as we did for custom attributes, as shown in the following code:

```
css_class = soup.find(attrs={'class':'primaryconsumerlist'})
print(css_class)

#output
<li class="primaryconsumerlist">
  <div class="name">deer</div>
  <div class="number">1000</div>
</li>
```

Since searching based on `class` is a common thing, Beautiful Soup has a special keyword argument that can be passed for matching the CSS class. The keyword argument that we can use is `class_` and since this is not a reserved keyword in Python, it won't throw an error.

Line 1:

```
css_class = soup.find(class_ = "primaryconsumers" )
```

Line 2:

```
css_class = soup.find(attrs={'class':'primaryconsumers'})
```

The preceding two code lines are same.

Searching using functions defined

We can pass functions to the `find()` method for searching based on the conditions defined within the function. The function should return a `true` or `false` value. The corresponding tag, as defined by the function, will be found by the `BeautifulSoup` object.

Let's take an example of finding the secondary consumers using functions within the `find()` method:

```
def is_secondary_consumers(tag):
   return tag.has_attr('id') and tag.get('id') ==
      'secondaryconsumers'
```

The function checks whether the tag has the `id` attribute and if its value is `secondaryconsumers`. If the two conditions are met, the function will return `true`, and so, we will get the particular tag we were looking for in the following code:

```
secondary_consumer =  soup.find(is_secondary_consumers)
print(secondary_consumer.li.div.string)

#output
fox
```

We use the `find()` method by passing the function that returns either `true` or `false`, and so, the tag for which the function returns `true` is displayed, which in our case, corresponds to the first secondary consumer.

Applying searching methods in combination

We saw how to search based on text, tag, attribute value, regular expression, and so on. Beautiful Soup also helps in searching based on the combination of any of these methods.

In the preceding example, we discussed searching based on the attribute value. It was easy since the attribute value was present on only one type of tag (for example, in `id='secondaryconsumers"`, the value was present only on the `<ul>` tag).

But, what if there were multiple tags with the same attribute value? For example, refer to the following code:

```
<p class="identical">
   Example of p tag with class identical
</p>
<div class="identical">
   Example of div tag with class identical
</div>
```

Here, we have a `div` tag and a `p` tag with the same class attribute value `"identical"`. In this case, if we want to search only for the `div` tag with the class attribute's value = `identical`, we can use a combination of search using a tag and attribute value within the `find()` method.

Let us see how we can search based on the preceding combination:

```
identical_div= soup.find("div",'class'_='identical')
print(identical_div)

#output
<div class="identical">
  Example of div tag with class identical
</div>
```

Similarly, we can have any combination of the searching methods.

Searching with find_all()

The `find()` method was used to find the first result within a particular search criteria that we applied on a `BeautifulSoup` object. As the name implies, `find_all()` will give us all the items matching the search criteria we defined. The different filters that we see in `find()` can be used in the `find_all()` method. In fact, these filters can be used in any searching methods, such as `find_parents()` and `find_siblings()`.

Let us consider an example of using `find_all()`.

Finding all tertiary consumers

We saw how to find the first and second primary consumer. If we need to find all the tertiary consumers, we can't use `find()`. In this case, `find_all()` will become handy.

```
all_tertiaryconsumers =
   soup.find_all(class_="tertiaryconsumerslist")
```

The preceding code line finds all the tags with the = "tertiaryconsumerlist" class. If given a type check on this variable, we can see that it is nothing but a list of tag objects as follows:

```
print(type(all_tertiaryconsumers))

#output
<class 'list'>
```

We can iterate through this list to display all tertiary consumer names by using the following code:

```
for tertiaryconsumer in all_tertiaryconsumers:
   print(tertiaryconsumer.div.string)
```

```
#output
lion
tiger
```

Understanding parameters used with find_all()

Like `find()`, the `find_all()` method also has a similar set of parameters with an extra parameter, `limit`, as shown in the following code line:

```
find_all(name,attrs,recursive,text,limit,**kwargs)
```

The `limit` parameter is used to specify a limit to the number of results that we get. For example, from the e-mail ID sample we saw, we can use `find_all()` to get all the e-mail IDs. Refer to the following code:

```
email_ids = soup.find_all(text=emailid_regexp)
print(email_ids)

#output
[u'abc@example.com',u'xyz@example.com',u'foo@example.com']
```

Here, if we pass `limit`, it will limit the result set to the limit we impose, as shown in the following example:

```
email_ids_limited = soup.find_all(text=emailid_regexp,limit=2)
print(email_ids_limited)

#output
[u'abc@example.com',u'xyz@example.com']
```

From the output, we can see that the result is limited to two.

> The `find()` method is `find_all()` with `limit=1`.

We can pass `True` or `False` values to find the methods. If we pass `True` to `find_all()`, it will return all tags in the `soup` object. In the case of `find()`, it will be the first tag within the object. The `print(soup.find_all(True))` line of code will print out all the tags associated with the `soup` object.

In the case of searching for text, passing `True` will return all text within the document as follows:

```
all_texts = soup.find_all(text=True)
print(all_texts)

#output
[u'\n', u'\n', u'\n', u'\n', u'\n', u'plants', u'\n', u'100000',
  u'\n', u'\n', u'\n', u'algae', u'\n', u'100000', u'\n', u'\n',
   u'\n', u'\n', u'\n', u'deer', u'\n', u'1000', u'\n', u'\n',
    u'\n', u'rabbit', u'\n', u'2000', u'\n', u'\n', u'\n',
     u'\n', u'\n', u'fox', u'\n', u'100', u'\n', u'\n', u'\n',
      u'bear', u'\n', u'100', u'\n', u'\n', u'\n', u'\n',
       u'\n', u'lion', u'\n', u'80', u'\n', u'\n', u'\n',
        u'tiger', u'\n', u'50', u'\n', u'\n', u'\n', u'\n',
         u'\n']
```

The preceding output prints every text content within the soup object including the new-line characters too.

Also, in the case of text, we can pass a list of strings and `find_all()` will find every string defined in the list:

```
all_texts_in_list = soup.find_all(text=["plants","algae"])
print(all_texts_in_list)

#output
[u'plants', u'algae']
```

This is same in the case of searching for the tags, attribute values of tag, custom attributes, and the CSS class.

For finding all the `div` and `li` tags, we can use the following code line:

```
div_li_tags = soup.find_all(["div","li"])
```

Similarly, for finding tags with the `producerlist` and `primaryconsumerlist` classes, we can use the following code lines:

```
all_css_class =
  soup.find_all(class_=["producerlist","primaryconsumerlist"])
```

Both `find()` and `find_all()` search an object's descendants (that is, all children coming after it in the tree), their children, and so on. We can control this behavior by using the `recursive` parameter. If `recursive = False`, search happens only on an object's direct children.

Search Using Beautiful Soup

For example, in the following code, search happens only at direct children for `div` and `li` tags. Since the direct child of the `soup` object is `html`, the following code will give an empty list:

```
div_li_tags = soup.find_all(["div","li"],recursive=False)
print(div_li_tags)

#output
[]
```

If `find_all()` can't find results, it will return an empty list, whereas `find()` returns `None`.

Searching for Tags in relation

Searching for contents within an HTML page is easy using the `find()` and `find_all()` methods. During complex web scraping projects, it will be very easy for a user to visit the subsequent tags or the parent tags for extra information.

These tags that we intend to visit will be in a direct relationship with the tag we already searched. For example, we may need to find the immediate parent tag of a particular tag. Also, there will be situations to find the previous tag, next tag, tags that are in the same level (siblings), and so on. In these cases, there are searching methods provided within the `BeautifulSoup` object, for example, `find_parents()`, `find_next_siblings()`, and so on. Normally, we use these methods followed by a `find()` or `find_all()` method since these methods are used for finding one particular tag and we are interested in finding the other tags, which are in relation with this tag.

Searching for the parent tags

We can find the parent tags associated with a tag by using the `find_parents()` or `find_parent()` methods. Likewise, `find_all()` and `find()` differ only in the number of results they return. The `find_parents()` method returns the entire matching parent tags, whereas `find_parent()` returns the first immediate parent. The searching methods that we discussed in `find()` can be used for `find_parent()` and `find_parents()`.

In the primary consumer example, we can find the immediate parent tag associated with `primaryconsumer` as follows:

```
primaryconsumers = soup.find_all(class_="primaryconsumerlist")
primaryconsumer = primaryconsumers[0]
parent_ul = primaryconsumer.find_parents('ul')
print(parent_ul)
```

```
#output
<ul id="primaryconsumers">

  <li class="primaryconsumerlist">

    <div class="name">deer</div>

    <div class="number">1000</div>

  </li>

  <li class="primaryconsumerlist">

    <div class="name">rabbit</div>

    <div class="number">2000</div>

  </li>

</ul>
```

The first line will store all the primary consumers in the `primaryconsumers` variable. We take the first entry and store that in `primaryconsumer`. We are trying to find all the `<ul>` tags, which are the parent tags of the `primaryconsumer` list that we got. From the preceding output, we can understand that the result will contain the whole structure of the parent, which will also include the tag for which we found the parent. We can use the `find_parent()` method to find the immediate parent of the tag.

```
parent_p = primaryconsumer.find_parent("p")
```

The preceding code will search for the first `<p>` tag, which is the immediate parent of the `<li>` tag with the `primaryconsumerlist` class in the ecological pyramid example.

An easy way to get the immediate parent tag for a particular tag is to use the `find_parent()` method without any parameter as follows:

```
immediateprimary_consumer_parent = primary_consumer.find_parent()
```

The result will be the same as `primary_consumer.find_parent('ul')` since ul is the immediate parent tag.

Searching for siblings

In a particular `html` document, we can say that particular tags are siblings, if they are at the same level. For example, in the ecological pyramid, all of the `<ul>` tags are on the same level and they are siblings if we define a relationship. We can understand this from the following diagram, which is a representation of the relationship between the first `div` tag and the `ul` tags:

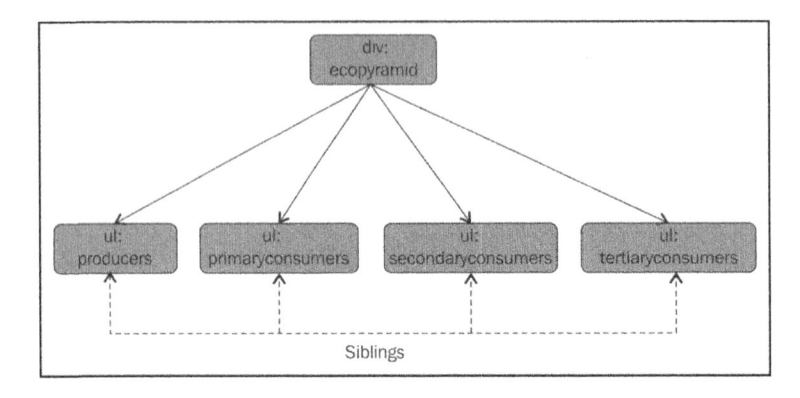

This means that in our example, the `ul` tags with the classes `producers`, `primaryconsumers`, `secondaryconsumers`, and `teritiaryconsumers` are siblings.

Also, in the following diagram for producers, we can see that the `plants` value, which is the first producer and `algae`, which is the second producer, cannot be treated as siblings, since they are not at the same level:

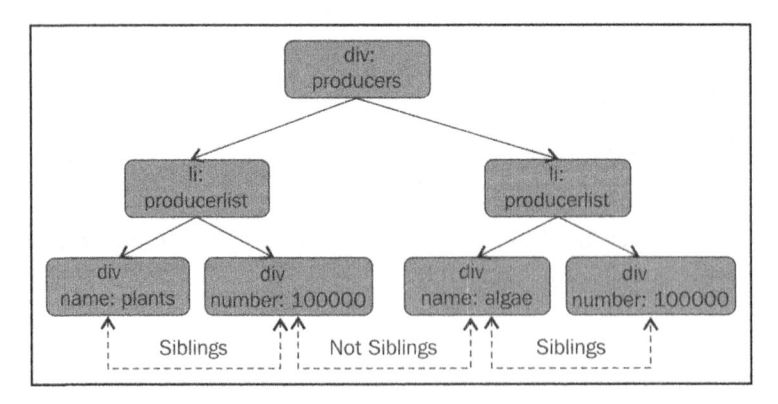

But, both `div` with the value `plants` and the value for number `10000` can be considered as siblings, as they are at the same level.

Chapter 3

Beautiful Soup comes with methods to help us find the siblings too.

The `find_next_siblings()` method allows to find the next siblings, whereas `find_next_sibling()` allows to find the next sibling. In the following example, we can find out the siblings of the producers:

```
producers= soup.find(id='producers')
next_siblings = producers.find_next_siblings()
print(next_siblings)

#output
[<ul id="primaryconsumers">

  <li class="primaryconsumerlist">

    <div class="name">deer</div>

    <div class="number">1000</div>

  </li>

  <li class="primaryconsumerlist">

    <div class="name">rabbit</div>

    <div class="number">2000</div>

  </li>

</ul>, <ul id="secondaryconsumers">

  <li class="secondaryconsumerlist">

    <div class="name">fox</div>

    <div class="number">100</div>

  </li>

  <li class="secondaryconsumerlist">

    <div class="name">bear</div>
```

[43]

```
        <div class="number">100</div>
      </li>
  </ul>, <ul id="tertiaryconsumers">
    <li class="tertiaryconsumerlist">
        <div class="name">lion</div>
        <div class="number">80</div>
    </li>
    <li class="tertiaryconsumerlist">
        <div class="name">tiger</div>
        <div class="number">50</div>
    </li>
  </ul>]
```

So, we find the next siblings for the producer, which are the primary consumers, secondary consumers, and tertiary consumers.

We can use `find_previous_siblings()` and `find_previous_sibling()` to find the previous siblings and previous sibling respectively.

Like other find methods, we can have the different filters such as text, regular expression, attribute value, and tag name to pass to these methods to find the siblings accordingly.

Searching for next

For every tag, there will be a next element that can either be a navigable string, `Tag` object, or any other `BeautifulSoup` object. By next element, we mean the element that is parsed immediately after the current element. This is different from a sibling. We have methods to find the next objects for a particular `Tag` object. The `find_all_next()` method helps to find all the objects coming after the tag and `find_next()` finds the first object that comes after the `Tag` object. In this method, we can also use the different search methods as in `find()`.

For example, we can find all the `li` tags that come after the first `div` tag using the following code:

```
first_div = soup.div
all_li_tags = first_div.find_all_next("li")

#output
[<li class="producerlist">
   <div class="name">plants</div>
   <div class="number">100000</div>
</li>, <li class="producerlist">
   <div class="name">algae</div>
   <div class="number">100000</div>
</li>, <li class="primaryconsumerlist">
   <div class="name">deer</div>
   <div class="number">1000</div>
</li>, <li class="primaryconsumerlist">
   <div class="name">rabbit</div>
   <div class="number">2000</div>
</li>, <li class="secondaryconsumerlist">
   <div class="name">fox</div>
   <div class="number">100</div>
</li>, <li class="secondaryconsumerlist">
   <div class="name">bear</div>
   <div class="number">100</div>
</li>, <li class="tertiaryconsumerlist">
   <div class="name">lion</div>
   <div class="number">80</div>
</li>, <li class="tertiaryconsumerlist">
   <div class="name">tiger</div>
   <div class="number">50</div>
</li>]
```

Searching for previous

Searching for `previous` is the opposite case of `next`, where we can find the previous object associated with a particular object. We can use the `find_all_previous()` method to find all the previous objects associated with the current object and `find_previous()` to find the previous object associated with the current object.

Search Using Beautiful Soup

Using search methods to scrape information from a web page

In *Chapter 2, Creating a BeautifulSoup Object*, we discussed the fetching of information related to all books published by Packt Publishing available at the link `http://www.packtpub.com/books`. In the following exercise, we will use Beautiful Soup searching methods to scrape all books from the preceding URL. We will scrape the name of the book, published date, and price from the preceding URL.

The first step involved in this exercise is to analyze the HTML document and to understand its logical structure. This will help us to understand how the required information is stored within the HTML document.

We can use the Google Chrome developer tools to understand the logical structure of the page. Let us do that by performing the following steps:

1. Open the page in the Google Chrome browser.
2. Right-click on it and select the **Inspect Element** option.
3. Now, we can see the **Developer tools** window at the bottom of the page.

The previous URL content under Google Chrome developer tool will be shown as follows for a particular book title:

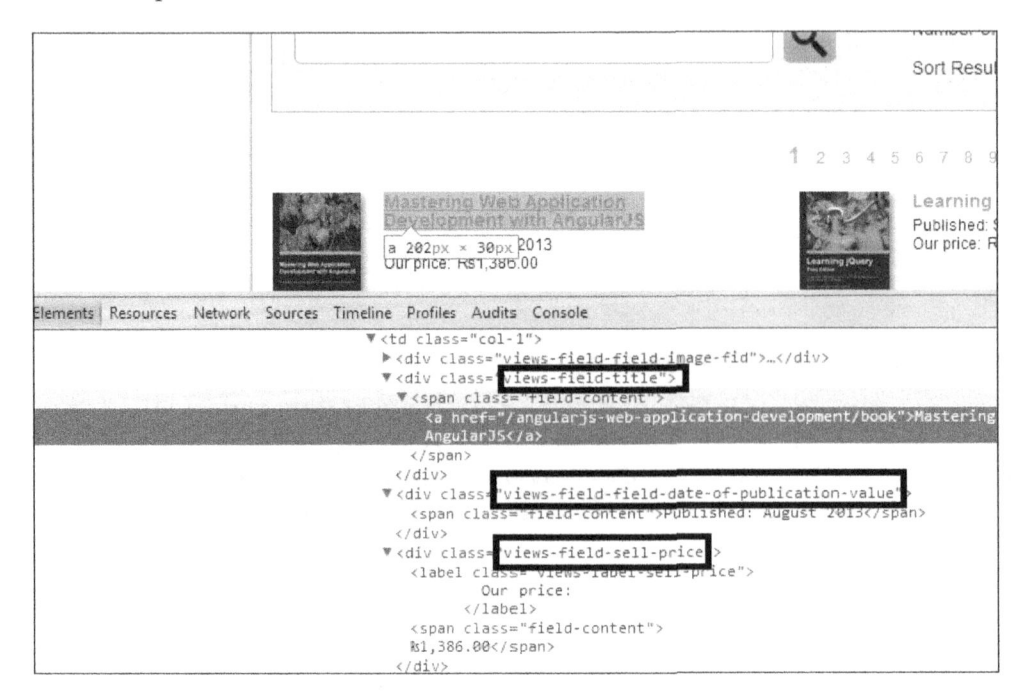

> The preceding screenshot is the representation of the previous URL at the time of writing this book. Since this is an online page, the data will be updated at regular intervals.

We can see that every book title is stored under a `<span>` tag with `class="field-content"`. If we take a closer look, we can see that both the published date information and the price information is stored inside a similar `<span>` tag with `class="field-content"`. In order to uniquely identify the preceding data, we can't take the `<span>` tag since all the three pieces of information are stored under the `<span>` tag with the same class. So, it will be better to identify another tag that encloses each piece of information uniquely. In this case, we can see that the `<span>` tag corresponding to the book title is stored inside a `<div>` tag with `class="views-field-title"`. Similarly, for published data information, the corresponding `<span>` tag is stored inside a `<div>` tag with `class=" views-field-field-date-of-publication-value"`. Likewise, the `<span>` tag for price is stored inside the `<div>` tag with `class="views-field-sell price"`. From the web page source, we can see that the structure is as follows and it supports the findings that we had:

```
<div class="views-field-title">
  <span class="field-content">
    <a href="/angularjs-web-application-development/book">
      Mastering Web Application Development with AngularJS</a>
  </span>
</div>
<div class="views-field-field-date-of-publication-value">
  <span class="field-content">Published: August 2013</span>
</div>
<div class="views-field-sell-price">
  <label class="views-label-sell price">
    Our price:
  </label>
  <span class="field-content">
    1,386.00</span>
</div>
```

Search Using Beautiful Soup

This is same for each book title in the page. Further analysis of the page shows that all the book titles are wrapped inside a table with `class="views-view-grid"`, as shown in the following screenshot:

So, we have formed the logical structure for finding all the books in the web page.

The next step is to form a parsing strategy based on the logical structure we found out. For the preceding case, we can form a parsing strategy as follows:

1. Find the table with `class="views-view-grid"`. This is the starting point since every book title is stored inside this table.

2. After getting the `Tag` object corresponding to the table, we should now search for all the book titles within this table. For titles, we should search for the `div` tag with `class = "views-field-title"`. From the logical structure, we can see that we should get the string inside the first `<a>` tag of the `<span>` tag, which is inside the `<div>` tag we searched for.

3. To find the published date for the corresponding book title, we should search for the next `div` tag with `class="views-field-field-date-of-publication-value"`. From the logical structure, we can see that for published date, we should get the string inside the `span` tag.

4. To find the price of the corresponding title, we should search for the next `div` tag with `class=" views-field-sell-price"`. From the logical structure, we can see that for the published date also, we should get the string inside the `span` tag.

We can apply the preceding parsing strategy for all the titles within the page. The next step is to convert this into a script so that we get all information related to the book title from the page.

We will first create the `BeautifulSoup` object based on the web page by taking the example from the previous chapter as follows:

```
import urllib2
from bs4 import BeautifulSoup
url = "http://www.packtpub.com/books"
page = urllib2.urlopen(url)
soup_packtpage = BeautifulSoup(page)
page.close()
```

First, we will search for the table with `class="views-view-grid"` as follows:

```
all_books_table = soup_packtpage.find("table",class_="views-view-
   grid")
```

Then, we will search for all the `div` tags with the `views-field-title` class within this `table` tag as follows:

```
all_book_titles = all_books_table.find_all("div",class_="views-
   field-title")
```

As next step, we will iterate through these tag objects, which represent the book title, and will find the published date and price for each title as follows:

```
for book_title in all_book_titles:
  book_title_span = book_title.span
  print("Title Name is :"+book_title_span.a.string)
  published_date = book_title.find_next("div",class_="views-field-
    field-date-of-publication-value")
  print("Published Date is :"+published_date.span.string)
    price = book_title.find_next("div",class_="views-field-sell-
      price")
  print("Price is :"+price.span.string)

#output
Title Name is :Mastering Web Application Development with AngularJS
```

Search Using Beautiful Soup

```
Published Date is :Published: August 2013
Price is :
1,386.00
Title Name is :Building Machine Learning Systems with Python
Published Date is :Published: July 2013
Price is :
1,540.00
Title Name is :Beginning Yii [Video]
Published Date is :Published: April 2012
Price is :
1,078.00
Title Name is :Responsive Web Design with HTML5 and CSS3
Published Date is :Published: April 2012
Price is :
1,232.00
Title Name is :jQuery UI 1.8: The User Interface Library for jQuery
Published Date is :Published: August 2011
Price is :
1,386.00
......
```

In the preceding script, we print the title of the book by getting the string inside the a tag, which is inside the first span tag. We searched for the next <div> tag by using find_next("div",class_="views-field-field-date-of-publication-value") to get the published date information. Similarly, for price, we used find_next("div",class_="views-field-sell-price"). The published date and price information was stored as a string of the first span tag and so, we used span.string to print this information. We will get all the book titles, published date, and price from the web page at http://www.packtpub.com/books by running the preceding script.

> We have created the program based on the HTML structure of the current page. The HTML code of this page can change over the course of time resulting in a change of the logical structure and parsing strategy.

Quick reference

Here, we will see the following searching methods in Beautiful Soup:

- `find()`: This function is used to find the first occurrence
- `find('p')`: This function is used to find the first occurrence of a tag
- `find(text="newtext")`: This function is used to find the first occurrence of text
- `find(attrs={'id':'value'})`: This function is used to find the first occurrence of attributes based on the attribute value
- `find(class_='value')`: This function is used to find the first occurrence with the CSS class value
- `find_all()`: This function is used to find all occurrences based on filter conditions
- `find_parent()`: This function is used to find the first occurrence in parent tags
- `find_parents()`: This function is used to find all occurrences in parent tags
- `find_sibling()`: This function is used to find the first occurrence in sibling tags
- `find_siblings()`: This function is used to find all occurrences in sibling tags
- `find_next()`: This function is used to find the first occurrence of a tag parsed immediately after the current tag
- `find_all_next()`: This function is used to find occurrences of all tags parsed immediately after the current tag
- `find_previous()`: This function is used to find the first occurrence of a tag parsed immediately before the current tag
- `find_all_previous()`: This function is used to find occurrences of all tags parsed immediately before the current tag

Summary

In this chapter, we dealt with the various search methods in Beautiful Soup, such as `find()`, `find_all()`, and `find_next()`. The different parameters that can be used with these methods were also explained with the help of sample code. Combinations of the different filters for the search methods and also finding the tags in relationships were also discussed in this chapter. We also looked at forming the logical structure and parsing strategy for finding all the information related to the book title from an online web page using the different search methods.

In the next chapter, we will learn the different navigation methods in Beautiful Soup.

4
Navigation Using Beautiful Soup

In *Chapter 3, Search Using Beautiful Soup*, we saw how to apply searching methods to search tags, texts, and more in an HTML document. Beautiful Soup does much more than just searching. Beautiful Soup can also be used to navigate through the HTML/XML document. Beautiful Soup comes with attributes to help in the case of navigation. We can find the same information up to some level using the searching methods, but in some cases due to the structure of the page, we have to combine both searching and navigation mechanisms to get the desired result. Navigation techniques come in handy in those cases. In this chapter, we will get into navigation using Beautiful Soup in detail.

Navigation using Beautiful Soup

Navigation in Beautiful Soup is almost the same as the searching methods. In navigating, instead of methods, there are certain attributes that facilitate the navigation. As we already saw in *Chapter 2, Creating a BeautifulSoup Object*, Beautiful Soup uses a different `TreeBuilder` to build the HTML/XML tree. So each `Tag` or `NavigableString` object will be a member of the resulting tree with the Beautiful Soup object placed at the top and other objects as the nodes of the tree.

The following code snippet is an example for an HTML tree:

```
html_markup = """<div class="ecopyramid">
  <ul id="producers">
    <li class="producerlist">
      <div class="name">plants</div>
      <div class="number">100000</div>
    </li>
```

```
      <li class="producerlist">
        <div class="name">algae</div>
        <div class="number">100000</div>
      </li>
    </ul>
  </div>"""
```

For the previous code snippet, the following HTML tree is formed:

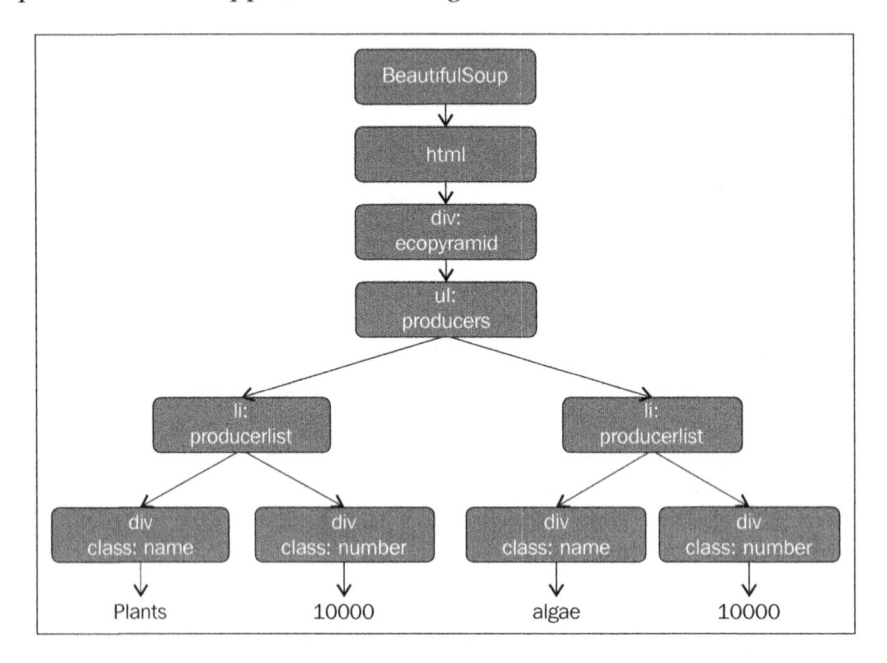

In the previous figure, we can see that Beautiful Soup is the root of the tree, the `Tag` objects make up the different nodes of the tree, while `NavigableString` objects make up the leaves of the tree.

Navigation in Beautiful Soup is intended to help us visit the nodes of this HTML/XML tree. From a particular node, it is possible to:

- Navigate down to the children
- Navigate up to the parent
- Navigate sideways to the siblings
- Navigate to the next and previous objects parsed

We will be using the previous `html_markup` as an example to discuss the different navigations using Beautiful Soup.

Navigating down

Any object, such as `Tag` or `BeautifulSoup`, that has children can use this navigation. Navigating down can be achieved in two ways.

Using the name of the child tag

A `BeautifulSoup` or a `Tag` object can use the name of a child tag to navigate to it. Even if there are multiple child nodes with the same name, this method will navigate to the first instance only. For example, we can consider the `BeautifulSoup` object on the ecological pyramid example discussed in the previous example.

```
soup = BeautifulSoup(html_markup,"lxml")
producer_entries = soup.ul
print(producer_entries)
```

In the previous code, by using `soup.ul`, we navigate to the first entry of the `ul` tag within the soup object's children.

This can also be done for `Tag` objects by using the following code:

```
first_producer = producer_entries.li
print(first_producer)

#output
<li class"="producerlist">
  <div class"="name">plants</div>
  <div class"="number">100000</div>
</li>
```

The previous code used navigation on the tag object, `producer_entries`, to find the first entry of the `<li>` tag. We can verify this from the output. But this cannot be used on a `NavigableString` object, as it doesn't have any children.

```
producer_name = first_producer.div.string
```

Here we stored the `NavigableString` plants in `producer_name`. Trying to navigate down from `producer_name` will result in an error.

```
producer_name.li
```

This will throw the following `AttributeError` since `NavigableString` can't have any child objects:

```
AttributeError: 'NavigableString' object has no attribute 'li'
```

Using predefined attributes

Beautiful Soup stores children in predefined attributes. There are two types of children.

- **Direct children**: These come immediately after a node in an HTML tree. For example, in the following figure, **html** is the direct child of **BeautifulSoup**.

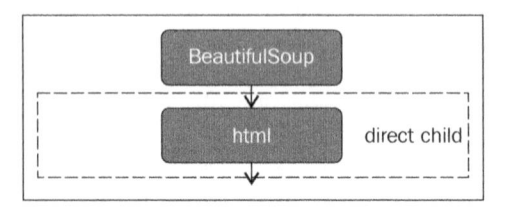

- **Descendants**: These contain all the children of a particular node including the direct child. For example, in the following image, we can see the direct child and the descendants of **BeautifulSoup**.

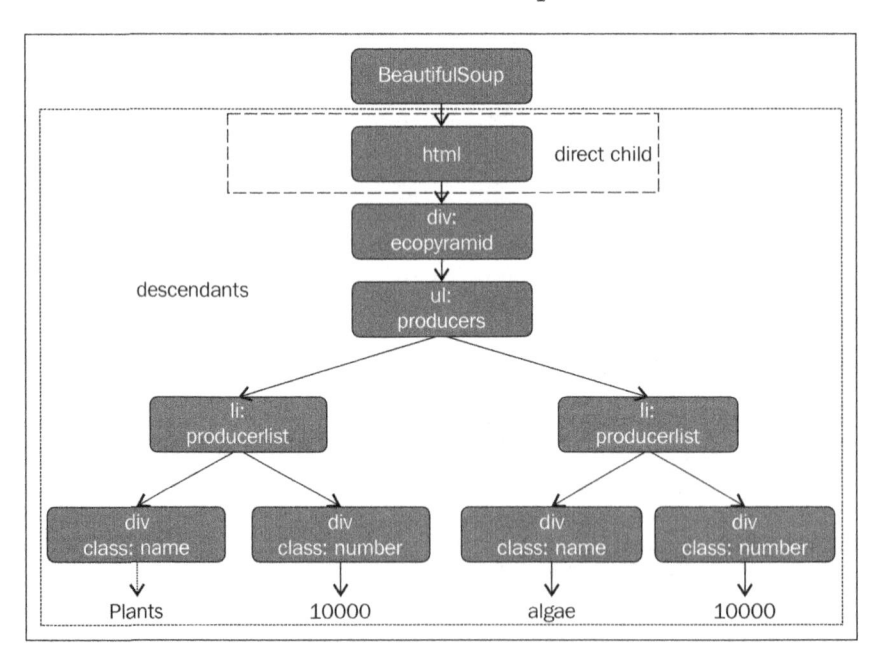

Descendants include all tags coming under Beautiful Soup.

Based on the previous categorization, there are the following different attributes for navigating to the children:

- .contents
- .children
- .descendants

These attributes will be present in all `Tag` objects and the `BeautifulSoup` object that facilitates navigation to the children.

The .contents attribute

The children of a `Tag` object or a `BeautifulSoup` object are stored as a list in the attribute `.contents`.

```
print(type(soup.contents))
#output
<class 'list'>
```

From the output, we know that `type` is a list that holds the children. In this case, the number of children of the `BeautifulSoup` object can be understood from the following code snippet:

```
print len(soup.contents)

#output
1
```

We can use any type of list navigation in Python on `.contents` too. For example, we can print the name of all children using the following code:

```
for tag in soup.contents:
    print(tag.name)

#output
html
```

Now let us see that in the case of the `Tag` object `producer_entries` using the following code snippet:

```
for child in producer_entries.contents:
  print(child)
#output
<li class="producerlist">
  <div class="name">plants</div>
  <div class="number">100000</div>
```

[57]

```
    </li>
    <li class="producerlist">
      <div class="name">algae</div>
      <div class="number">100000</div>
```

The .children attribute

The `.children` attribute is almost the same as the `.contents` attribute. But it is not a list like `.contents`, instead it is a Python generator and we can iterate over this to get each child.

```
print type(soup.children)

#output
<class 'list_generator'>
```

We can iterate over `.children` of the `BeautifulSoup` object, and get the children as in the example code given as follows:

```
for tag in soup.children:
   print(tag.name)

#output
html
```

The .descendants attribute

The `.contents` and `.children` attributes consider the immediate children only, that is, `soup.contents` or `soup.children` returned only the root HTML tag.

Navigation to all children of a particular object is possible using `.descendants`.

```
print(len(list(soup.descendants)))
#output
13
```

From the output, we can see that `.descendants` gives 13, whereas `.contents` or `.children` gave only 1.

Now let us print all descendants in this case.

```
from bs4.element import NavigableString
for tag in soup.descendants:
   if isinstance(tag, NavigableString):
     print(tag)
   else:
     print(tag.name)
```

```
#output
html
body
p
ul
li
div
plants
div
100000
li
div
algae
div
100000
```

Here we are iterating through all the descendants of the `soup` object. Since `NavigableString` doesn't have the `.Name` attribute, we are checking it and printing the string itself in the previous code. But for a Tag object, we just print the `.name` attribute.

The output for the code is entirely different from the ones in which we used `.contents` or `.children`.

Special attributes for navigating down

Getting text data within a particular tag is one of the common use cases in scraping. Beautiful Soup provides special attributes to navigate to the string contained within each Tag object using the attributes `.string` and `.strings`.

The .string attribute

If a tag has `NavigableString` as the only child or if it has another tag that has a `NavigableString` object as a child, we can navigate to `NavigableString` using the `.string` attribute. As we know, `NavigableString` represents the text stored inside the tag; using `.string`, we navigate to the text stored inside the tag.

```
first_producer = soup.div
print(first_producer.string)

#output
plants
```

The .strings attribute

Even if there are multiple child objects comprising of string and other tags, we can still get the string of each child using the `.strings` generator. In the previous example, we have the `<li>` tag with two `<div>` tags as children. These `<div>` tags contain strings. We can get these strings from the parent `<li>` tag using the `.strings` generator, which is shown as follows:

```
for string in li.strings:
  print(string)
#output
plants
10000
```

Navigating up

Like navigating down to find children, Beautiful Soup allows users to find the parents of a particular `Tag/NavigableString` object. Navigating up is done using `.parent` and `.parents`.

The .parent attribute

From the first figure, we understand that all `Tag` and `NavigableString` objects have a parent. The parent of a particular `Tag` object can be found using the attribute `.parent`.

```
producer_entries = soup.ul
print(producer_entries.parent)

#output
div
```

The `.parent` attribute of the top most `<html>`/`<xml>` tag is the `BeautifulSoup` object itself.

```
html_tag = soup.html
print(html_tag.parent.name)

#output
u'[document]'
```

Since the `soup` object is at the root of the tree, it didn't have a parent. So `.parent` on the `soup` object will return `None`.

```
print(soup.parent)

#output
None
```

The .parents attribute

The `.parents` attribute is a generator that holds parents of a particular `Tag`/`NavigableString`.

```
third_div = soup.find_all("div")[2]
```

In the previous code, we store the third `<div>` entry, which is `<div class"="name">algae</div>` in `third_div`.

Using this we iterate through the parents of this tag.

```
for parent in third_div.parents:
  print(parent.name)
#output

li
ul
body
html
[document]
```

In the previous code, we navigate to the `<li>` tag, which is the immediate parent object of `third_div`, then to the `<ul>` tag, which is the parent of the `<li>` tag. Likewise, navigation to the `html` tag and finally `[document]`, which represents the `soup` object, is done.

Navigating sideways to the siblings

Apart from navigating through the content up and down the HTML tree, Beautiful Soup also provides navigation methods to find the siblings of an object. Navigating to the siblings is possible using `.next_sibling` and `.previous_sibling`.

Navigation Using Beautiful Soup

The .next_sibling attribute

In the producer list, we can get the sibling of the first producer `plants` using the following code snippet:

```
soup = BeautifulSoup(html_markup)
first_producer = soup.find("li")
second_producer = first_producer.next_sibling
second_producer_name = second_producer.div.string
print(second_producer_name)

#output
u'algae'
```

Here `second_producer` is reached by navigating to the next sibling from `first_producer`, which represents the first `<li>` tag within the page.

The .previous_sibling attribute

The `.previous_sibling` attribute is used to navigate to the previous sibling. For finding the previous sibling in the previous example, we can use the following code snippet:

```
print(second_producer.previuos_sibling)

#output
<li class="producerlist"><div class="name">plants</div><div
  class="number">100000</div></li>
```

If a tag doesn't have a previous sibling, it will return `None`, that is `print(first_producer.previous_sibling)` will give us `None` since there are no previous sibling for this tag.

We have `next_siblings` and `previous_siblings` generators to iterate over the next and previous siblings from a particular object.

```
for previous_sibling in second_producer.previous_siblings:
  print(previous_sibling.name)
```

The previous code snippet will give only the `<li>` tag, which is the only previous sibling. The same iteration can be used for `next_siblings` to find the siblings coming after an object.

Navigating to the previous and next objects parsed

We saw different ways of navigating to the children, siblings, and parents. Sometimes we may need to navigate to objects that may not be in direct relation with the tag such as the children, siblings, or parent. So, in order to find the immediate element that is parsed after, our object can be found using `.next_element`.

For example, the immediate element parsed after the first `<li>` tag is the `<div>` tag.

```
first_producer = soup.li
print(first_producer.next_element)

#output
<div class="name">plants</div>
```

The previous code prints the next element, which is `<div class="name">plants</div>`.

> `.next_element` and `.next_sibling` are entirely different. `.next_element` points to the object that is parsed immediately after the current object, whereas `.next_sibling` points to the object that is at the same level in the tree.

In the same way, `.previous_element` can be used to find the immediate element parsed before a particular tag or string.

```
second_div = soup.find_all("("div")[")[1]
print(second_div.previous_element)

#output
plants
```

From the output, it is clear that the one parsed immediately before the second `<div>` tag is the string `plants`.

Quick reference

The following commands will help you to navigate down the tree:

- `tag.name`: This navigates to the child using the name
- `tag.contents`: This lists the children
- `tag.children`: This is a generator for children

- `tag.descendants`: This is a generator for descendants
- `tag.string`: This navigates to a string using `.string`
- `tag.strings`: This is a generator for strings

The following commands will help you to navigate up the tree:

- `tag.parent`: This navigates to the parent
- `tag.parents`: This is a generator for parents

The following commands will help you to navigate sideways:

- `tag.next_sibling`: This navigates to the next sibling
- `tag.next_siblings`: This is a generator for next siblings
- `tag.previous_sibling`: This navigates to the previous sibling
- `tag.previous_siblings`: This is a generator for previous siblings

The following commands help you to navigate to the previous or next element:

- `tag.next_element`: This navigates to the next element parsed
- `tag.previous_element`: This navigates to the previous element parsed

Summary

In this chapter, we discussed the various navigation techniques in Beautiful Soup. We have discussed four ways of navigation, that is, navigating up, down, sideways, next, and before elements with the help of examples.

In the next chapter, we will learn about the different ways to modify the parsed HTML tree by adding new contents, for example, tags, strings, modifying tags, and deleting existing ones.

5
Modifying Content Using Beautiful Soup

Beautiful Soup can be used effectively to search or navigate within an HTML/XML document. Apart from this, we can also use Beautiful Soup to change the content of an HTML/XML document. Modification of the content means the addition or deletion of a new tag, changing the tag name, altering tag attribute values, changing text content, and so on. This is useful in situations where we need to parse the HTML/XML document, change its structure, and write it back as an HTML/XML document with the modification.

Consider a case where we have an HTML document with a `<table>` tag holding around 1,000 or more rows (the `<tr>` tag) with an existing set of two columns (the `<td>` tag) per row. We want to add a new set of the two `<td>` tags to each row. It would be highly inappropriate to manually add these `<td>` tags for each of the `<tr>` tags. In this case, we can use Beautiful Soup to search or/and navigate through each of the `<tr>` tags to add these `<td>` tags. We can then save these changes as a new HTML document, which will then have the four `<td>` tags per `<tr>` tag. This chapter deals with the different methods to modify content using Beautiful Soup by considering the ecological pyramid example that we used in the previous chapters.

Modifying Tag using Beautiful Soup

Beautiful Soup has the capability of altering completely different properties of the HTML/XML tags. We know that each tag in Beautiful Soup is represented as a `Tag` object and it is possible to perform the following tasks:

- Modifying the name property of `Tag`
- Modifying the attribute values of `Tag`
- Adding new tags

- Deleting existing tags
- Modifying string contents

Modifying the name property of Tag

A Beautiful Soup `Tag` object is always associated with a `.name` property; for example, `a`, `div`, and so on. Modifying the `.name` property with a new value will modify the HTML tag as follows:

```
html_markup = """<div class="ecopyramid">
<ul id="producers">
  <li class="producerlist">
    <div class="name">plants</div>
    <div class="number">100000</div>
  </li>
  <li class="producerlist">
    <div class="name">algae</div>
    <div class="number">100000</div>
  </li>
</ul>"""

soup = BeautifulSoup(html_markup,"lxml")
producer_entries = soup.ul
print(producer_entries.name)

#output
'ul'
```

From the preceding output, we can see that `producer_entries` has the name `ul`; we can easily change this by modifying the `.name` property.

The representation of the HTML tree is given in the following diagram:

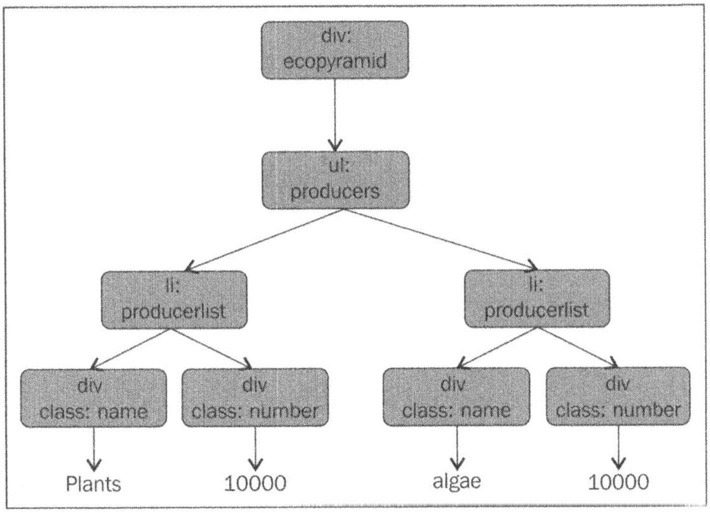
div:
ecopyramid
ul:
producers
li:
producerlist
li:
producerlist
div
class: name
div
class: number
div
class: name
div
class: number
Plants
10000
algae
10000

Let us modify the value to `div`, as shown in the following code:

```
producer_entries.name = "div"
print(producer_entries.prettify())

#output
<html>
  <body>
    <div class="ecopyramid">
    <div id="producers">
      <li class="producerlist">
        <div class="name">
          plants
        </div>
        <div class="number">
          100000
          </div>
        </li>
        <li class="producerlist">
          <div class="name">
            algae
          </div>
          <div class="number">
            100000
```

```
            </div>
          </li>
        </div>
     </div>
   </body>
</html>
```

This also causes the HTML tree to change as shown in the following diagram:

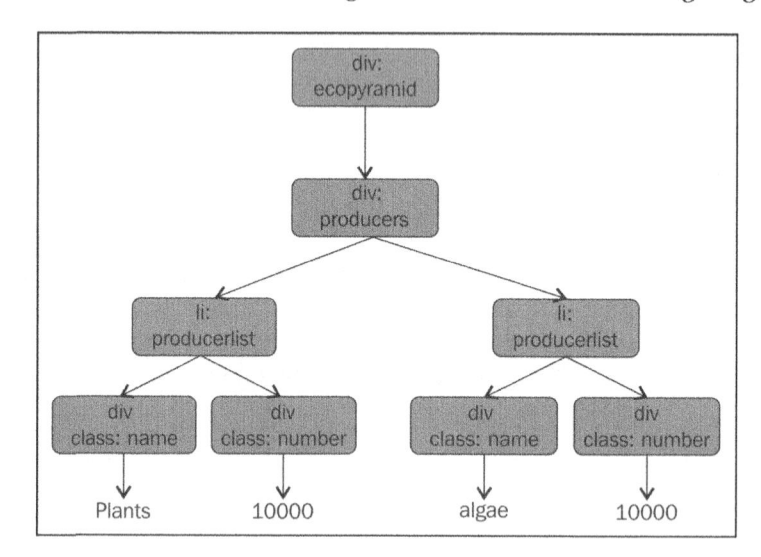

[Diagram: div: ecopyramid → div: producers → two li: producerlist nodes, each with div class: name and div class: number children, leading to "Plants", "10000", "algae", "10000"]

We can use the `prettify()` method to show the formatted output, as shown in the preceding code. As we can see, changing the `Tag` object's name property also changes the HTML tree. So, we should be careful when renaming the tags since it can lead to malformed HTML tags.

Modifying the attribute values of Tag

Beautiful Soup can also be used to modify the attribute values associated with a tag such as `class`, `id`, and `style`. Since the attributes are stored as a dictionary, it is as simple as dealing with a normal Python dictionary.

Updating the existing attribute value of Tag

In the previous ecological pyramid example, the ul tag has the id attribute with the value producers. We can change this value to producers_new_value as follows:

```
producer_entries['id']="producers_new_value"
```

Now, if we print the `producer_entries` object, we can see the change in place as follows:

```
print(producer_entries.prettify())

#output
<div id="producers_new_value">
  <li class="producerlist">
    <div class="name">
      plants
    </div>
    <div class="number">
      100000
    </div>
  </li>
  <li class="producerlist">
    <div class="name">
      algae
    </div>
    <div class="number">
      100000
    </div>
  </li>
</div>
```

Adding new attribute values to Tag

We can add a new attribute to a `Tag` object. In the previous example, the `ul` tag doesn't have a class attribute. We can add this as follows:

```
producer_entries['class']='newclass'
```

The preceding code will add the new attribute if it doesn't exist or will update the attribute value if the attribute already existed in the HTML tree.

```
print(producer_entries.prettify())
#output
<div class="newclass" id="producers_new_value">
  <li class="producerlist">
    <div class="name">
      plants
    </div>
    <div class="number">
      100000
    </div>
```

```
      </li>
      <li class="producerlist">
        <div class="name">
          algae
        </div>
        <div class="number">
          100000
        </div>
      </li>
    </div>
```

From the preceding output, we can verify that the new `class` attribute is being added to the HTML tree.

Deleting the tag attributes

In the preceding example, we have added a new tag attribute to the `ul` tag. Beautiful Soup also allows deleting any of the tag attributes. Since the tag attributes are stored as a dictionary in Python, it is enough to use the `del` operator that is used to delete items in a Python dictionary as follows:

```
del producer_entries['class']
```

The preceding code will remove the attribute class associated with the `ul` tag. Refer to the following code:

```
print(producer_entries.prettify())

#output
<div id="producers_new_value">
  <li class="producerlist">
    <div class="name">
      plants
    </div>
    <div class="number">
      100000
    </div>
  </li>
  <li class="producerlist">
    <div class="name">
      algae
    </div>
    <div class="number">
      100000
```

```
      </div>
   </li>
</div>
```

Adding a new tag

We've seen some of the different ways to change the `Tag` object's `.name` property and to modify the `Tag` attributes. Beautiful Soup also allows us to add a new tag to the existing HTML/XML document. The `new_tag()` method creates a new tag within the `soup` object. We can then add these tags to the tree by using either the `append()`, `insert()`, `insert_after()`, or `insert_before()` method.

Adding a new producer using new_tag() and append()

In our ecological pyramid example, we already have `plants` and `algae` as the producers. Let us add one more producer to the HTML, for example, `phytoplankton`. If we analyze the HTML, we can see that we need to first add a `li` tag to the parent `ul` tag. For this, we need to create the `li` tag first.

Creating a new tag using new_tag()

The Beautiful Soup's `new_tag()` method will help us to create a new tag. The `new_tag()` method can be called only on the `BeautifulSoup` object. So, here we need to create a new tag, `li`, with the `producerlist` class. For this, refer to the following code:

```
soup = BeautifulSoup(html_markup,"lxml")
new_li_tag = soup.new_tag("li")
```

The preceding code will create and store the new `li` tag in the `new_li_tag` variable. The `new_tag()` method requires only the tag name as mandatory. We can pass attribute values or other properties as optional parameters. That is, we can have the following code:

```
new_atag=soup.new_tag("a",href="www.example.com")
```

In the preceding example, we created the `<a>` tag by giving a name as well as the `href` property and its value.

It is also possible to add a new attribute value to the previously created `li` tag using the following code:

```
new_li_tag.attrs={'class':'producerlist'}
```

Adding a new tag using append()

We have created the li tag but we need to fix it to the correct position. Beautiful Soup allows us to add a tag to another tag or the soup object using the append() method. The append() method adds a newly created tag to the end of .contents. This can be called in the same way as the append() method in a Python list as follows:

```
producer_entries = soup.ul
producer_entries.append(new_li_tag)
```

The preceding code will append the newly created li tag to .contents of the ul tag. So, the li tag will now be the child of the ul tag. The ul tag structure will look like the following code:

```
print(producer_entries.prettify())

#output
<ul id="producers">
  <li class="producerlist">
    <div class="name">
      plants
    </div>
    <div class="number">
      100000
    </div>
  </li>
  <li class="producerlist">
    <div class="name">
      algae
    </div>
    <div class="number">
      100000
    </div>
  </li>s
  <li class="producerlist">
  </li>
</ul>
```

From the preceding output, we can see that the newly created li tag is added as the new child of ul. Now, we have to add the two div tags inside this li tag.

[72]

Adding a new div tag to the li tag using insert()

Like `append()`, the `insert()` method can also be used to add a new tag into the HTML tree. As we already know, `append()` adds a newly created tag to the end of `.contents`. But, `insert()` on the other hand, doesn't insert at the end of `.contents`; instead, we need to specify the position at which the tag has to be inserted. This is the same as the list `insert()` operation in Python. Refer to the following code:

```
new_div_name_tag=soup.new_tag("div")
new_div_name_tag["class"]="name"
new_div_number_tag=soup.new_tag("div")
new_div_number_tag["class"]="number"
```

The preceding lines of code will create the two new `div` tags with the corresponding `class` attributes as follows:

```
new_li_tag.insert(0,new_div_name_tag)
new_li_tag.insert(1,new_div_number_tag)
print(new_li_tag.prettify())

#output
<li class_="producerlist">
  <div class="name">
  </div>
  <div class="number">
  </div>
</li>
```

Now, we can see that new tags have been inserted into the `li` tags. But, the respective strings are missing in these tags.

Modifying string contents

In the preceding example, we added the two `div` tags without any contents to the HTML tree. We need to add the corresponding string in the `name` property of the `div` tag and also into the `number` property of the `div` tag. This can also be done in multiple ways using Beautiful Soup.

Using .string to modify the string content

We can use the `.string` attribute of a tag to modify the string content. So, we can add or modify the string value using the following code:

```
new_div_name_tag.string="phytoplankton"
print(producer_entries.prettify())

#output
<ul id="producers">
  <li class="producerlist">
    <div class="name">
      plants
    </div>
    <div class="number">
      100000
    </div>
  </li>
  <li class="producerlist">
    <div class="name">
      algae
    </div>
    <div class="number">
      100000
    </div>
  </li>
  <li class="producerlist">
    <div class="name">
      phytoplankton
    </div>
    <div class="number">
    </div>
  </li>
</ul>
```

We can see that the string has been added in the preceding code example.

Adding strings using .append(), insert(), and new_string()

We can add more strings to the existing tag using the `.append()` or `.insert()` method. They behave in the same way as in adding a new tag. In the case of string contents, the `append()` method appends to the end of `.string`, whereas the `insert()` method inserts to the specific position of `.string`. For example, we can add a new string to the `name` property of the `div` tag using the following code:

```
new_div_name_tag.append("producer")
print(soup.prettify())

#output
<html>
  <body>
    <div class="ecopyramid">
      <ul id="producers">
        <li class="producerlist">
          <div class="name">
            plants
          </div>
          <div class="number">
            100000
          </div>
        </li>
        <li class="producerlist">
          <div class="name">
            algae
          </div>
          <div class="number">
            100000
          </div>
        </li>
        <li class="producerlist">
          <div class="name">
            phytoplankton
            producer
          </div>
          <div class="number">
          </div>
        </li>
      </ul>
```

Modifying Content Using Beautiful Soup

```
      </div>
   </body>
</html>
```

There is one more method, `new_string()`, that will help in creating a new string as follows:

```
new_string_toappend = soup.new_string("producer")
new_div_name_tag.append(new_string_toappend)
```

The preceding code will create the new string and now, we can use either `append()` or `insert()` to add the newly created string to the tree.

Like `append()`, we can also use `insert()` for inserting strings as follows:

```
new_string_toinsert  =soup.new_string("10000")
new_div_number_tag.insert(0,new_string_toinsert)
```

The resulting tree after the addition of the producer will look like the following code:

```
<html>
  <body>
    <div class="ecopyramid">
      <ul id="producers">
        <li class="producerlist">
          <div class="name">
            plants
          </div>
          <div class="number">
            100000
          </div>
        </li>
        <li class="producerlist">
          <div class="name">
            algae
          </div>
          <div class="number">
            100000
          </div>
        </li>
        <li class_="producerlist">
          <div class_="name">
            phytoplankton
            producer
          </div>
          <div class="number">
```

```
            10000
        </div>
      </li>
    </ul>
  </div>
 </body>
</html>
```

Deleting tags from the HTML document

Beautiful Soup also allows for the removal of tags from the document. This is accomplished using the `decompose()` and `extract()` methods.

Deleting the producer using decompose()

We have added the new producer, `phytoplankton`.

We can remove this producer entry by removing the `div` tags first and then the `li` tags from the `ul` tag. We will remove the `div` tag with `class="name"` using the `decompose()` method.

```
third_producer = soup.find_all("li")[2]
div_name = third_producer.div
div_name.decompose()
print(third_producer.prettify())

#output
<li class_="producerlist">
  <div class_="number">
    10000
  </div>
</li>
```

In the preceding code, we have used `find_all()` to find all the `li` entries and we stored the third producer into the `third_producer` variable. Then, we found the first `div` tag and removed it using the `decompose()` method.

> The `decompose()` method is used to remove the tag from an HTML/XML document. It will remove the tag and its children.

Modifying Content Using Beautiful Soup

Likewise, we can remove the `div` tag with the `class="number"` entry too. Refer to the following code:

```
third_producer = soup.find_all("li")[2]
div_number= third_producer.div
div_number.decompose()
print(third_producer.prettify())

#output

  <li class="producerlist">
  </li>
```

Deleting the producer using extract()

We have removed both the `div` tags from the `li` tag using the `decompose()` method. The removal of the `div` tag itself doesn't guarantee the removal of the third producer; for this, we need to remove the `li` tag also. We can do that using the `decompose()` method as well. But, Beautiful Soup has one more method that helps in the removal of a tag.

The `extract()` method is used to remove a tag or string from an HTML tree. Additionally, it also returns a handle to the tag or string removed. Unlike `decompose()`, the extract can be used in strings as well. This is shown as follows:

```
third_producer_removed=third_producer.extract()
print(soup.prettify())

#output
<html>
  <body>
    <div class="ecopyramid">
      <ul id="producers">
        <li class="producerlist">
          <div class="name">
            plants
          </div>
          <div class="number">
            100000
          </div>
        </li>
        <li class="producerlist">
          <div class="name">
```

```
              algae
            </div>
            <div class="number">
              100000
            </div>
          </li>
        </ul>
      </div>
    </body>
</html>
```

After executing the preceding code, we can see that the third producer, which is `phytoplankton`, has been removed from the ecological pyramid example.

Deleting the contents of a tag using Beautiful Soup

Tags can either have a `NavigableString` object or Tag objects as children. Removal of these child objects can be done by using `clear()`.

For example, we can remove the `<div>` tags holding `plants` and the corresponding `<div>` with the class number from the `li` tag using the `clear()` method; this is shown as follows:

```
li_plants=soup.li
```

Since it is the first `li` tag, we will be able to select it using the name; this is shown as follows:

```
li_plants.clear()
```

This will remove all `.contents` of the tag. So, `clear()` will remove all the strings and the children within a particular tag. This is shown as follows:

```
print(li_name)

#output
<li class="producerlist"></li>
```

[79]

Special functions to modify content

Apart from the methods we saw before, Beautiful Soup has the following other methods for modifying the content:

- The `insert_after()` and `insert_before()` methods:

    As the name implies, these methods are used to insert a tag or string after or before another tag or string. The only parameter accepted by this method is the `NavigavleString` or `Tag` object.

    For example, we can add another `div` tag with `class=ecosystem` to the ecological pyramid example using `insert_after()`. To use this, we need to first find the `div` tag with `class=number` within the first producer `li`; this is shown as follows:

    ```
    soup = BeautifulSoup(html_markup,"lxml")
    div_number = soup.find("div",class_="number")
    div_ecosystem = soup.new_tag("div")
    div_ecosystem['class'] = "ecosystem"
    div_ecosystem.append("soil")
    div_number.insert_after(div_ecosystem)
    print(soup.prettify())

    #output
    <html>
      <body>
        <div class="ecopyramid">
          <ul id="producers">
            <li class="producerlist">
              <div class="name">
                plants
              </div>
              <div class="number">
                100000
              </div>
              <div class="ecosystem">
                soil
              </div>
            </li>
            <li class="producerlist">
              <div class="name">
                algae
              </div>
    ```

```
            <div class="number">
                100000
            </div>
        </li>
    </ul>
  </div>
 </body>
</html>
```

Here, we have created a new `div` tag and appended the string `soil` to it. We used the `insert_after()` method to insert the tag in the correct place. Likewise, we can use `insert_before()` to insert a `Tag` or `NavigableString` object before something else in the tree.

- The `replace_with()` method:

  The `replace_with()` method is used to replace a tag or a string with a new tag or a string within the document. The `replace_with()` method will accept either a tag or a string object as input. For example, we can change the string of the first producer to `phytoplankton` using the `replace_with()` method. The `replace_with()` method will return the tag or string that was replaced.

```
soup = BeautifulSoup(html_markup,"lxml")
div_name =soup.div
div_name.string.replace_with("phytoplankton")
print(soup.prettify())

#output
<html>
  <body>
    <div class="ecopyramid">
      <ul id="producers">
        <li class="producerlist">
          <div class="name">
            phytoplankton
          </div>
          <div class="number">
            100000
          </div>
          <div class="ecosystem">
            soil
          </div>
        </li>
```

```
            <li class="producerlist">
              <div class="name">
                algae
              </div>
              <div class="number">
                100000
              </div>
            </li>
          </ul>
        </div>
      </body>
    </html>
```

The `replace_with()` method can also be used to replace a tag completely.

- The `wrap()` and `unwrap()` methods:

    The `wrap()` method is used to wrap a tag or string with another tag that we pass. For example, we can wrap the entire contents in the `li` tag with another `<div>` tag in our following example:

```
li_tags = soup.find_all("li")
for li in li_tags:
  new_divtag = soup.new_tag("div")
  li.wrap(new_divtag)
print(soup.prettify())
#output
<html>
  <body>
    <div class="ecopyramid">
      <ul id="producers">
        <div>
          <li class="producerlist">
            <div class="name">
              phytoplankton
            </div>
            <div class="number">
              100000
            </div>
            <div class="ecosystem">
              soil
            </div>
          </li>
        </div>
        <div>
```

```
            <li class="producerlist">
              <div class="name">
                algae
              </div>
              <div class="number">
                100000
              </div>
            </li>
          </div>
        </ul>
      </div>
    </body>
</html>
```

From the preceding output, it is clear that we wrapped the li tag with another div tag.

The unwrap() method does the opposite of wrap() and is used to unwrap the contents as follows:

```
soup = BeautifulSoup(html_markup,"lxml")
li_tags = soup.find_all("li")
for li in li_tags:
  li.div.unwrap()
print(soup.prettify())

#output
<html>
  <body>
    <div class="ecopyramid">
      <ul id="producers">
        <li class="producerlist">
          plants
          <div class="number">
            100000
          </div>
          <div class="ecosystem">
            soil
          </div>
        </li>
      </div>
      <div>
        <li class="producerlist">
          algae
```

```
                <div class="number">
                    100000
                </div>
            </li>
        </div>
    </ul>
  </div>
 </body>
</html>
```

Here, the first `div` tag will be unwrapped, that is, the `div` tag with `class="name"`.

> The `unwrap()` method, such as `replace_with()`, will return the tag that was replaced.

Quick reference

You can take a look at the following references to get an overview of the modifying content:

- Modifying the `Tag` name:

    The following code line modifies the name property:

    - `tag.name = "newvalue"`: This line of code modifies the `Tag` name as `newvalue`

- Modifying the `Tag` attribute:

    The following code lines alter the attributes:

    - `tag["attr"] = "newvalue"`: This line of code modifies the `Tag` attribute
    - `del tag["attr"]`: This line of code deletes the `Tag` attribute

- Adding new tags:

    The following code lines correspond to the addition of content:

    - `newtag = soup.new_tag('tagname')`: This line of code creates `newtag`
    - `oldtag.append(newtag)`: This line of code appends `newtag` to `oldtag.contents`
    - `oldtag.insert(0,newtag)`: This line of code inserts `newtag` at the index 0 of `oldtag.contents`

- Modifying the `string` contents:

    The following code lines are used to modify the `string` content:

    - `tag.string = "helloworld"`: This line of code modifies `tag.string`
    - `tag.append("helloworld")`: This line of code appends `"helloworld"` to the existing `tag.string`
    - `newstring= soup.new_string("helloworld")`: This line of code creates a new `NavigableString` object
    - `tag.insert(0,newstring)`: This line of code inserts `newstring` at the index `0` of `tag.string`

- Deleting the existing tags:

    The following code lines help to remove the existing tag attributes:

    - `tag.decompose()`: This line of code removes a tag and its children
    - `tag.extract()`: This line of code removes and returns a tag or string
    - `tag.clear()`: This line of code removes children

- Special functions:

    The following are the special functions used to add or alter tags:

    - `oldtag.insert_after(newtag)`: This function inserts `newtag` after `oldtag`
    - `oldtag.insert_before(newtag)`: This function inserts `newtag` before `oldtag`
    - `oldtag.replace_with(newtag)`: This function replaces `oldtag` with `newtag`
    - `oldtag.wrap(newtag)`: This function wraps `oldtag` with `newtag`
    - `oldtag.unwrap(newtag)`: This function unwraps `newtag` within `oldtag`

Summary

In this chapter, we took a look at the content modification techniques in Beautiful Soup. The creation and addition of new tags and the modification of attribute values were discussed with the help of an example. The deletion and replacing of content was also explained. Finally, we dealt with some special functions, such as `replace_with()`, `wrap()`, and `unwrap()`, which are very helpful when it comes to dealing with changing the contents.

In the next chapter, we will discuss the encoding support in Beautiful Soup.

6
Encoding Support in Beautiful Soup

All web pages will have an encoding associated with it. Modern websites have different encodings such as UTF-8, and Latin-1. Nowadays, UTF-8 is the encoding standard used in websites. So, while dealing with the scraping of such pages, it is important that the scraper should also be capable of understanding those encodings. Otherwise, the user will see certain characters in the web browser whereas the result you would get after using a scraper would be gibberish characters. For example, consider a sample web content from Wikipedia where we are able to see the Spanish character ñ.

Alphabet [edit]

The Spanish language is written using the Spanish alphabet, which is the Latin alphabet with one additional letter, eñe (ñ), for a total of 27 letters.[1] Although the letters (k) and (w) are part of the alphabet, they appear only in loanwords such as *karate*, *kilo*, *waterpolo* and *wolframio* 'tungsten'. Each letter has a single official name according to the Real Academia Española's new 2010 Common Orthography,[1] but in some regions alternative traditional names coexist as explained below.

Spanish Alphabet

Letter	A	B	C[1]	D	E	F	G	H	I
Name	a	be, be larga, be alta	ce	de	e	efe	ge	hache	i
IPA	/a/	/b/	/k/, /θ/[2]	/d/	/e/	/f/	/g/, /x/	silent[3]	/i/
Letter	J	K	L	M	N	Ñ	O	P	Q
Name	jota	ka	ele	eme	ene	eñe	o	pe	cu
IPA	/x/	/k/	/l/[4]	/m/	/n/	/ɲ/	/o/	/p/	/k/[5]
Letter	R[6]	S	T	U	V	W	X	Y	Z
Name	erre	ese	te	u	ve, uve, ve corta, ve baja	uve doble, ve doble, doble ve, doble u[2]	equis	i griega, ye	zeta
IPA	/r/, /ɾ/	/s/	/t/	/u/	/b/	/gw/, /b/	/ks/, /x/, /s/	/j/, /i/	/θ/[2]

^1 The sequence (ch) represents the affricate /tʃ/. The digraph was formerly treated as a single letter, called *che*.

Encoding Support in Beautiful Soup

If we run the same content through a scraper with no support for the previous encoding used by the website, we might end up with the following content:

```
The Spanish language is written using the Spanish alphabet, which
   is the Latin alphabet with one additional letter,
   e&#21336;e (&#21336;), for a total of 27 letters.
```

We see the Spanish character ñ is replaced with gibberish characters. So it is important that a scraper should support different encodings. Beautiful Soup handles these encodings pretty neatly. In this chapter, we will see the encoding support in Beautiful Soup.

Encoding in Beautiful Soup

As already explained, every HTML/XML document will be written in a specific character set encoding, for example, UTF-8, and Latin-1. In an HTML page, this is represented using the `meta` tag as shown in the following example:

```
<meta http-equiv="Content-Type" content="text/html;charset=UTF-8">
```

Beautiful Soup uses the `UnicodeDammit` library to automatically detect the encoding of the document. Beautiful Soup converts the content to Unicode while creating `soup` objects from the document.

> Unicode is a character set, which is a list of characters with unique numbers. For example, in the Unicode character set, the number for the character B is 42. UTF-8 encoding is an algorithm that is used to convert these numbers into a binary representation.

In the previous example, Beautiful Soup converts the document to Unicode.

```
html_markup = """<p> The Spanish language is written using the
   Spanish alphabet, which is the Latin alphabet  with one
   additional letter, eñe (ñ), for a total of 27 letters.</p>
"""
soup = BeautifulSoup(html_markup,"lxml")
print(soup.p.string)

#output
The Spanish language is written using the Spanish alphabet, which
   is the Latin alphabet with one additional letter, e单e (单), for
   a total of 27 letters.
```

From the previous output, we can see that there is a difference in the additional letter part (e単e (単)) because there is a gibberish character instead of the actual representation. This is due to the wrong interpretation of the original encoding in the document by `UnicodeDammit`.

Understanding the original encoding of the HTML document

The previous HTML content was originally of UTF-8 encoding. But Beautiful Soup, while generating the `soup` object, detects encoding using the `UnicodeDammit` library and we can get hold of this original encoding using the attribute `original_encoding`.

The `soup.original_encoding` will give us the original encoding, which is `euc-jp` in the previous case. This is wrong because `UnicodeDammit` detected the encoding as `euc jp` instead of `utf-8`.

Specifying the encoding of the HTML document

The `UnicodeDammit` library detects the encoding after a careful search of the entire document. This is time consuming and there are cases where the `UnicodeDammit` library detects the encoding as wrong, as observed previously. This wrong guess happens mostly when the content is very short and there are similarities between the encodings. We can avoid these if we know the encoding of the HTML document upfront. We can pass the encoding to the `BeautifulSoup` constructor so that the excess time consumption and wrong guesses can be avoided. The encoding is specified as a part of the constructor in the `from_encoding` parameter. So in the previous case, we can specify the encoding as `utf-8`.

```
soup = BeautifulSoup(html_markup,"lxml",from_encoding="utf-8")
print(soup.prettify())

#output
<html>
  <body>
    <p>
      The Spanish language is written using the Spanish alphabet,
        which is the Latin alphabet with one additional letter,
        eñe (ñ), for a total of 27 letters.
    </p>
  </body>
</html>
```

Encoding Support in Beautiful Soup

There are no longer gibberish characters because we have specified the correct encoding and we can verify this from the output.

The encoding that we pass should be correct, otherwise the character encoding will be wrong; for example, if we pass the encoding as `latin-1` in the preceding HTML fragment, the result will be different.

```
soup = BeautifulSoup(html_markup,"lxml",from_encoding="latin-1")
print(soup.prettify())

#output
'The Spanish language is written using the Spanish alphabet, which
   is the Latin alphabet with one additional letter, e͍e (单), for
   a total of 27 letters.
```

So it is better to pass the encoding only if we are sure about the encoding used in the document.

Output encoding

Encoding support is also present for the output text from Beautiful Soup. There are certain output methods in Beautiful Soup, for example, `prettify()`, which will give the output only in the UTF-8 encoding. Even though the encoding was something different like `ISO 8859-2`, the output will be in UTF-8. For example, the following HTML content is an example of ISO8859-2 encoding:

```
html_markup = """
<html>
  <meta http-equiv="Content-Type"
    content="text/html;charset=ISO8859-2"/>
  <p>cédille (from French), is a hook or tail ( ž )  added under
    certain letters as a diacritical mark to modify their
    pronunciation
  </p>"""
soup = BeautifulSoup(html_markup,"lxml")
```

The `soup.original_encoding` will give us the encoding as `ISO8859-2`, which is true for the preceding HTML code snippet. But `print (soup.prettify())` will give the output in `utf-8`.

```
<html>
  <head>
    <meta content="text/html;charset=utf-8" http-equiv="Content-
      Type"/>
```

```
      </head>
      <body>
        <p>
          cÄšdille (from French), is a hook or tail ( Ĺž ) added under
            certain letters as a diacritical mark to modify their
            pronunciation
        </p>
      </body>
</html>
```

Note that the `meta` tag got changed to `utf-8` to reflect the changes; also, the characters are different from the original content.

This is the default behavior of the `prettify()` method. But if we don't want the encoding to be changed to UTF-8, we can specify the output encoding by passing it in the `prettify()` method as shown in the following code snippet:

```
print(soup.prettify("ISO8859-2")
```

The preceding code line will give the output in ISO8859-2 itself.

```
<html>
  <head>
    <meta content="text/html;charset=ISO-8859-2" http-
      equiv="Content-Type"/>
  </head>
  <body>
    <p>
      cédille (from French), is a hook or tail ( ž ) added under
        certain letters as a diacritical mark to modify their
        pronunciation
    </p>
  </body>
</html>
```

We can also call `encode()` on any Beautiful Soup object and represent it in the encoding we pass. The `encode()` method also considers UTF-8 encoding by default. This is shown in the following code snippet:

```
print(soup.p.encode())

#output
cÄšdille (from French), is a hook or tail ( Ĺž ) added under
  certain letters as a diacritical mark to modify their
  pronunciation
```

Like `prettify()`, `encode()` also takes a different encoding as its parameter.

```
print(soup.encode("ISO-8859-2")

#output
cédille (from French), is a hook or tail ( ž ) added under certain
   letters as a diacritical mark to modify their pronunciation
```

Quick reference

You can take a look at the following references to get an overview of the code present in this chapter:

- `soup = BeautifulSoup(html_markup,"lxml",from_encoding="latin-1")`. Here, `from_encoding` is used while creating `BeautifulSoup` to specify the document encoding.
- `soup.original_encoding`: This gives the original encoding detected by Beautiful Soup.
- The output content in specific encoding is listed using the following methods:
    - `soup.prettify()`
    - `soup.encode()`

Summary

In this chapter, we saw the encoding support in Beautiful Soup. We understood how to get the original encoding detected by Beautiful Soup. We also learned to create a `BeautifulSoup` object by explicitly specifying the encoding. The output encoding was also discussed in this chapter. The next chapter deals with the different methods provided by Beautiful Soup to display content.

7
Output in Beautiful Soup

Beautiful Soup not only searches, navigates, and modifies the HTML/XML, but also the output content in a good format. Beautiful Soup can deal with different types of printing such as:

- Formatted printing
- Unformatted printing

Apart from these, Beautiful Soup provides different formatters to format the output. Since the HTML tree can undergo modification after creation, these output methods will help in viewing the modified HTML tree.

Also in this chapter, we will discuss a simple method of getting only the text stored within a web page.

Formatted printing

Beautiful Soup has two supported ways of printing. The first one is formatted printing that prints the current Beautiful Soup object into the formatted Unicode strings. Each tag is printed in a separate line with good indentation and this leads to the right look and feel. Beautiful Soup has the built-in method `prettify()` for formatted printing. For example:

```
html_markup = """<p class="ecopyramid">
<ul id="producers">
  <li class="producerlist">
    <div class="name">plants</div>
    <div class="number">100000</div>
  </li>
  <li class="producerlist">
    <div class="name">algae</div>
```

Output in Beautiful Soup

```
            <div class="number">100000</div>
        </li>
</ul>"""
soup = BeautifulSoup(html_markup,"lxml")
print(soup.prettify())
```

The following screenshot shows the output:

In the output, we can see that `<html><body>` gets appended. This is because Beautiful Soup uses the `lxml` parser and it identifies any string passed by default as HTML and performs the printing after appending the extra tags.

The `prettify()` method can be called either on a Beautiful Soup object or any of the tag objects. For example:

```
producer_entry = soup.ul
print(producer_entry.prettify())
```

Unformatted printing

Beautiful Soup supports the plain printing of the `BeautifulSoup` and `Tag` objects. This will return only the plain string without any formatting.

This can be done by using the `str()` or the `unicode()` method.

If we use the `str()` method on the `BeautifulSoup` or the `Tag` object, we get a normal Python string, shown as follows:

```
print(str(soup))

#output
'<html><body><p class="ecopyramid"></p><ul id="producers"><li
    class="producerlist"><div class="name">plants</div><div
    class="number">100000</div></li><li class="producerlist"><div
    class="name">algae</div><div
    class="number">100000</div></li></ul></body></html>'
```

We can use the `encode()` method that we used in *Chapter 6, Encoding Support in Beautiful Soup*, to encode the output in a specific encoding format.

We can use the `decode()` function on the `BeautifulSoup` or `Tag` object to get the Unicode string.

```
print(soup.decode())

#output
u'<html><body><p class="ecopyramid"></p><ul id="producers"><li
    class="producerlist"><div class="name">plants</div><div
    class="number">100000</div></li><li class="producerlist"><div
    class="name">algae</div><div
    class="number">100000</div></li></ul></body></html>'
```

Apart from this, Beautiful Soup supports different formatters to format the output.

Output formatters in Beautiful Soup

HTML entities are code that can be placed in an HTML file to represent special characters or symbols. These symbols are not generally present on the keyboard, and HTML entities are special code that render them when opened in a browser. For example, consider the following HTML:

```
<html>
  <body>
    <table>
      <tr>
        <th bgcolor="#ffffff">Symbols</th>
        <th bgcolor="#ffffff">Html Entity</th>
        <th bgcolor="#ffffff">Meaning</th>
      </tr>
      <tr>
```

```html
        <th>&amp;</th>
        <td align="center">&amp;amp;</td>
        <td align="center">ampersand</td>
     </tr>
     <tr>
        <th>&cent;</th>
        <td align="center">&amp;cent;</td>
        <td align="center">cent</td>
     </tr>
     <tr>
        <th>&copy;</th>
        <td align="center">&amp;copy;</td>
        <td align="center">copyright</td>
     </tr>
     <tr>
        <th>&#247;</th>
        <td align="center">&amp;divide;</td>
        <td align="center">divide</td>
     </tr>
     <tr>
        <th>&gt;</th>
        <td align="center">&amp;gt;</td>
        <td align="center">greater than</td>
     </tr>

   </table>
  </body>
</html>
```

This HTML code will look as shown in the following screenshot:

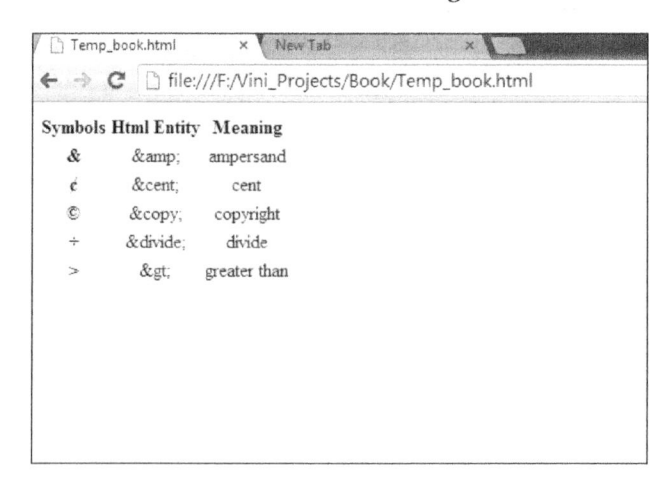

Symbols	Html Entity	Meaning
&	&amp;	ampersand
¢	&cent;	cent
©	&copy;	copyright
÷	&divide;	divide
>	&gt;	greater than

The left-most column represents the symbols and the corresponding HTML entities are represented in the next column. For the symbol &, the corresponding HTML entity code is & likewise for the symbol ©, the code is &copy.

The output methods in Beautiful Soup escape only the HTML entities of >, <, and & as >, <, and &. Rest of the special entities are converted to Unicode while constructing the BeautifulSoup object, and upon output using prettify() or other methods, we get only the UTF-8 string of the HTML entities. We won't get the HTML entities back (except for &, >, and <).

```
html_markup = """<html>
  <body>&    &amp;    ampersand
    ¢    &cent;   cent
    ©    &copy;   copyright
    ÷    &divide; divide
    >    &gt;     greater than
  </body>
</html>
"""
soup = BeautifulSoup(html_markup,"lxml")
print(soup.prettify())
```

Here we have created the soup object based on the text content for the HTML page in a browser that had the & symbol instead of the & code. Likewise for other entities in the prettify() method, the output is shown as follows:

```
>>> soup = BeautifulSoup(html_fragment)
>>> print soup.prettify()
<html>
 <body>
  &amp; &amp;   ampersand
  ¢      ¢      cent
  ©      ©      copyright
  ÷      ÷      divide
  &gt;   &gt;   greater than
 </body>
</html>
```

We can understand that other HTML entities were converted to Unicode representation. Beautiful Soup allows output formatters to have a control over this behavior. There are the following four types of formatters available:

- minimal
- html
- None
- function

We can pass different formatters as parameters to any of the output methods, such as `prettify()`, `encode()`, and `decode()`.

The minimal formatter

In this formatting mode, strings will be processed enough to generate a valid HTML code. This is the default formatter and the HTML entities that are escaped are `&amp;`, `&gt;` and `&lt;`. The output will be similar to the one shown in the previous screenshot.

The html formatter

In this formatting mode, Beautiful Soup will convert the Unicode characters to HTML entities.

```
print(soup.prettify(formatter="html"))
```

The following screenshot shows the difference between using the `minimal` and `html` formatters:

```
>>> print soup.prettify(formatter="minimal")
<html>
 <body>
   &amp;    &amp;    ampersand
   ¢        ¢        cent
   ©        ©        copyright
   ÷        ÷        divide
   &gt;     &gt;     greater than
 </body>
</html>
>>> print soup.prettify(formatter="html")
<html>
 <body>
   &amp;    &amp;    ampersand
   &cent;   &cent;   cent
   &copy;   &copy;   copyright
   &divide; &divide;          divide
   &gt;     &gt;     greater than
 </body>
</html>
```

From the previous screenshot we can identify that the formatter `html` changes whatever Unicode characters possible back to HTML entities.

The None formatter

In this case, Beautiful Soup will not modify the strings. This can lead to the generation of an invalid HTML code.

The `print(soup.prettify(formatter=None))` code line produces an output similar to the following screenshot:

```
>>> print soup.prettify(formatter=None)
<html>
 <body>
    &       &       ampersand
    ¢       ¢       cent
    ©       ©       copyright
    ÷       ÷       divide
    >       >       greater than
 </body>
</html>
```

The function formatter

We can specify a Python function and what to do with each string and attribute value.

```
def remove_chara(markup:
    return markup.replace("a","")
```

Here we define a function to remove the character a from the strings passed.

```
print(soup.prettify(formatter=remove_chara))
```

We use this function to strip out the a characters from the output. We should note that this will not escape the three special characters `&amp;`, `&gt;`, and `&lt;` in the output as shown in the following screenshot:

```
>>> print soup.prettify()
<html>
 <body>
    &amp; &amp;   ampersand
    ¢       ¢       cent
    ©       ©       copyright
    ÷       ÷       divide
    &gt;  &gt;    greater than
 </body>
</html>
>>> print soup.prettify(formatter=removeChara)
<html>
 <body>
    &       &       mpersnd
    ¢       ¢       cent
    ©       ©       copyright
    ÷       ÷       divide
    >       >       greter thn
 </body>
</html>
```

Output in Beautiful Soup

Using get_text()

Getting just text from websites is a common task. Beautiful Soup provides the method `get_text()` for this purpose.

If we want to get only the text of a Beautiful Soup or a `Tag` object, we can use the `get_text()` method. For example:

```
html_markup = """<p class="ecopyramid">
<ul id="producers">
  <li class="producerlist">
    <div class="name">plants</div>
    <div class="number">100000</div>
  </li>
  <li class="producerlist">
    <div class="name">algae</div>
    <div class="number">100000</div>
  </li>
</ul>"""
soup = BeautifulSoup(html_markup,"lxml")
print(soup.get_text())

#output
plants
100000

algae
100000
```

The `get_text()` method returns the text inside the Beautiful Soup or `Tag` object as a single Unicode string. But `get_text()` has issues when dealing with web pages. Web pages often have JavaScript code, and the `get_text()` method returns the JavaScript code as well. For example, in *Chapter 3, Search Using Beautiful Soup*, we saw the example of scraping book details from `packtpub.com`.

```
import urllib2
from bs4 import BeautifulSoup
url = "http://www.packtpub.com/books"
page = urllib2.urlopen(url)
soup_packtpage = BeautifulSoup(page,"lxml")
```

We can print the text inside the page using `get_text()`; this is shown in the following code snippet:

```
print(soup_packtpage.get_text())
```

With the previous code line, we will also get JavaScript code in the output as shown:

```
$(window).load(function() {
  $("img[data-original]").addClass("lazy");
  $("img.lazy").lazyload();
  setTimeout(function() {
    addthis_config = Drupal.settings.addthis.config_default;
      addthis_share = Drupal.settings.addthis.share_default;
    if (typeof pageTracker != "undefined")
      {addthis_config.data_ga_tracker = pageTracker;}
    var at = document.createElement("script"); at.type =
      "text/javascript"; at.async = true;
    at.src = "//dgdsbygo8mp3h.cloudfront.net/sites/default/
      files/addthis/addthis_widget.js";
    var s = document.getElementsByTagName("script")[0];
      s.parentNode.insertBefore(at, s);
  }, 5);

});
```

Removing the JavaScript and printing only the text within a document can be achieved using the following code line:

```
[x.extract() for x in soup_packtpage.find_all('script')]
```

The previous code line will remove all the script elements from the document. After this, the `print(soup_packtpage.get_text())` code line will print only the text stored within the page.

Quick reference

You can take a look at the following references to get an overview:

- Formatted printing: The following method gives the formatted output:
    - `soup.prettify()`: This method is used to output with indentation and formatting

- Unformatted printing: These methods give output without any format or indentation:
    - `str(soup)`
    - `soup.encode()`
    - `soup.decode()`

- Formatters: These methods have the ability to control the behavior of the output:
    - `soup.prettify(formatter="minimal")`
    - `soup.prettify(formatter="html")`
    - `soup.prettify(formatter="None")`
    - `soup.prettify(formatter=already_defined_func)`
- `get_text()`: This method gives you all the content of an object or a tag:
    - `soup.get_text()`: This method is used to get all the text content in `BeautifulSoup` or `Tag` objects

Summary

This chapter dealt with the different output methods in Beautiful Soup. We saw the formatted and unformatted printing in the `BeautifulSoup` object and also the different output formatters to control the output formatting. We also saw a method of getting only the text from a web page.

In the next chapter, we will create a web scraper using searching, navigation, and other techniques we have studied in this book so far.

Creating a Web Scraper

In this chapter, we will create a website scraper using the different searching and navigation techniques we studied in the previous chapters. The scraper will visit three websites to find the selling price of books based on the ISBN. We will first find out the book list and selling price from `packtpub.com`. We will also find the ISBN of the books from `packtpub.com` and search other websites such as `www.amazon.com` and `www.barnesandnoble.com` based on this ISBN. By doing this, we will automate the process of finding the selling price of the books on three websites and will also get a hands-on experience in implementing scrapers for these websites. Since the website structure may change later, the code examples and images used in this chapter may also become invalid. So, it is better to take the examples as a reference and change the code accordingly. It is good to visit these websites for a better understanding.

Getting book details from PacktPub.com

Getting book details from `www.packtpub.com` is the first step in the creation of the scraper. We need to find the following details from `PacktPub.com`:

- Book title name
- Selling price
- ISBN

We have seen how to scrape the book title and the selling price from `packtpub.com` in *Chapter 3, Search Using Beautiful Soup*. The example we discussed in that chapter considered only the first page and didn't include the other pages that also had the list of books. So in the next topic, we will find different pages containing a list of books.

Creating a Web Scraper

Finding pages with a list of books

The page at www.packtpub.com/books has the **next** and **previous** navigation links to go back and forth between the pages containing a list of books, as shown in the following screenshot:

So, we need to find out a method for getting multiple pages that contain the list of books. Logically, it seems to look at the page being pointed at by the next element in the current page. Taking a look at the next element, for page 49, using the Google Chrome developer tools, we can see that it actually points to the next page link, that is, /books?page=49. If we observe different pages using the Google Chrome developer tools, we can see that the link to the next page's actually has a pattern of /books?page=n for the n+1 page, that is, n=49 for the 50th page, as shown in the following screenshot:

From the preceding screenshot, we can further understand that the next element is within the `<li>` tag with class="pager-next last". Inside the `<li>` tag, there is an `<a>` tag that holds the link to the next page. In this case, the corresponding value is /books?page=49, which points to the 50th page. We have to add www.packtpub.com to this value to make a valid URL, as www.packtpub.com/books?page=49.

[104]

Chapter 8

If we analyze the `packtpub.com` website, we can see that the list of published books ends at page 50. So, we need to ensure that our program stops at this page. The program can stop looking for more pages if it is unable to find the next element.

For example, as shown in the following screenshot, for page 50, we don't have the next element:

So at this point, we can stop looking for further pages.

Our logic for getting pages should be as follows:

1. Start with the first page.
2. Check if it has a next element:
    - If yes, store the next page URL
    - If no, stop looking for further pages
3. Load page at URL and repeat the preceding step.

We can use the following code to find pages containing a list of books from `packtpub.com`:

```
import urllib2
import re
from bs4 import BeautifulSoup
packtpub_url = "http://www.packtpub.com/"
```

We stored `http://packtpub.com` in the `packtpub_url` variable. Each next element link should be prefixed with `packtpub_url` to form a valid URL, `http://www.packptpub.com/book?page=n`, as shown in the following code:

```
def get_bookurls(url):
    page = urllib2.urlopen(url)
    soup_packtpage = BeautifulSoup(page,"lxml")
```

```
      page.close()
      next_page_li = soup_packtpage.find("li", class_="pager-next
        last")
      if next_page_li is None :
        next_page_url = None
      else:
        next_page_url = packtpub_url+next_page_li.a.get('href')

      return next_page_url
```

The preceding `get_bookurls()` function returns the next page URL if we provide the current page URL. For the last page, it returns `None`.

In `get_bookurls()`, we created a BeautifulSoup object, `soup_packtpage`, based on the URL input and then searched for the `li` tag with the `pager-next last` class. If `find()` returns a tag, we can get the link to the next page using `next_page_li.a.get('href')`. We prefixed this value with `packtpub_url` and it is returned.

We need a list of such page URLs (for example www.packtpub.com/books, www.packtpub.com/books?page=2, and so on) to collect details of all the books on those pages.

In order to create this list to collect these details, use the following code:

```
    start_url = "www.packtpub.com/books"
    continue_scrapping = True
    books_url = [start_url]
    while continue_scrapping:
      next_page_url= get_bookurls(start_url)
      if next_page_url is None:
        continue_scraping = False
      else:
        books_url.append(next_page_url)
        start_url = next_page_url
```

In the preceding code, we started with the URL www.packtpub.com/books and stored it in the `books_url` list. We used a flag, `continue_scraping`, to control the execution of the function and we can see that the loop will terminate when `get_bookurls` returns `None`.

The `print(books_url)` entry prints the different URL from www.packtpub.com/books to www.packtpub.com/books?page=49.

Finding book details

Now, it is time for us to find the details of each book, such as the book title, selling price, and ISBN. The book title and selling price can be found from the main page with the list of books. But the ISBN can be found only on the details page of each book. So from the main pages, for example, www.packtpub.com/books, we have to find the corresponding link to fetch the details of each book.

We can use the following code to find the details of each book:

```
def get_bookdetails(url):
    page = urllib2.urlopen(url)
    soup_packtpage = BeautifulSoup(page,"lxml")
    page.close()
    all_books_table = soup_packtpage.find("table",class_="views-
       view-grid")
    all_book_titles =all_books_table.find_all("div",class_="views-
       field-title")
    isbn_list = []
    for book_title in all_book_titles:
       book_title_span = book_title.span
       print("Title Name:"+book_title_span.a.string)
       print("Url:"+book_title_span.a.get('href'))
       price = book_title.find_next("div",class_="views-field-sell-
          price")
       print("PacktPub Price:"+price.span.string)
       isbn_list.append(get_isbn(book_title_span.a.get('href')))
    return isbn_list
```

The preceding code is the same as the code we used in *Chapter 3, Search Using Beautiful Soup*, to get the book details. An addition is the use of `isbn_list` to hold the ISBN numbers and the `get_isbn` function that returns the ISBN for a particular book.

Creating a Web Scraper

The ISBN of a book is stored in the book's details page, as shown in the following screenshot:

In the preceding `get_bookdetails()` function, the `book_title_span.a.get('href')` function holds the URL to the details page of each book. We pass the preceding value to the `get_isbn()` function to get the ISBN.

The details page of a book when viewing through the developer tools has the ISBN, as shown in the following screenshot:

From the preceding screenshot, we can see that the **ISBN** number is stored as text followed by the ISBN inside the `b` tag.

Now, in the following code, let us see how we can find the ISBN using the `get_isbn()` function:

```
def get_isbn(url):
    book_title_url = packtpub_url + url
    page = urllib2.urlopen(book_title_url)
    soup_bookpage = BeautifulSoup(page,"lxml")
    page.close()
    isbn_tag = soup_bookpage.find('b',text=re.compile("ISBN :"))
    return isbn_tag.next_sibling
```

In the preceding code, we searched for the `b` tag with the text that matches the pattern `ISBN:`. The ISBN is `next_sibling` of the `b` tag.

In each main page, there will be a list of books, and for each book, there will be an ISBN. So we need to call the `get_bookdetails()` method for each of the `books_url` lists as follows:

```
isbns = []
for bookurl in books_url:
    isbns+= get_bookdetails(bookurl)
```

The `print(isbns)` function will print the list of ISBNs for all the books that are currently published by `packtpub.com`.

We scraped the selling price, book title, and ISBN from the PacktPub website. We will use the ISBN to search for the selling price of the same books in both `www.amazon.com` and `www.barnesandnoble.com`. With that, our scraper will be complete.

Getting selling prices from Amazon

We can search on Amazon for books based on their ISBNs. Normally, we will use the default search page on Amazon and enter the ISBN. We can do this manually, but from a program or scraper, we should know the URL to request based on the ISBN. Let us go to the Amazon site and search for this book with the ISBN, as shown in the following screenshot:

Creating a Web Scraper

The page generated after the search in Amazon will have a URL structure as follows:

`http://www.amazon.com/s/ref=nb_sb_noss?url=search-alias%3Daps&field-keywords=1783289554`

If we search based on another ISBN, that is, `http://www.amazon.com/s/ref=nb_sb_noss?url=search-alias%3Daps&field-keywords=1847195164`, we will see that it gives us back the details based on the **1847195164** ISBN.

From this, we can conclude that if we substitute `field-keywords` of the URL with the corresponding ISBN, we will be getting the details for that ISBN.

From the `http://www.amazon.com/s/ref=nb_sb_noss?url=search-alias%3Daps&field-keywords=1783289554` page, we have to find the selling price for the book. We can follow the same method to use the Google Chrome developer tools to see which tag holds the selling price.

From the preceding screenshot, we can see that the price is stored inside the `div` tag with the `newPrice` class. We can find the selling price from Amazon using the following code:

```
def get_sellingprice_amazon(isbn):
  url_foramazon =
    "http://www.amazon.com/s/ref=nb_sb_noss?url=search-
      alias%3Daps&field-keywords="
  url_for_isbn_inamazon = url_foramazon+isbn
  page = urllib2.urlopen(url_for_isbn_inamazon)
  soup_amazon = BeautifulSoup(page,"lxml")
```

```
page.close()
selling_price_tag = soup_amazon.find('div',class_="newPrice")
if selling_price_tag:
    print ("Amazon Price"+selling_price_tag.span.string)
```

We created the `soup` object based on the URL. After creating the `soup` object, we found the `div` tags with the `newPrice` class. The selling price is stored inside the `<span>` tag and we print it using `print (selling_price_tag.span.string)`.

Getting the selling price from Barnes and Noble

We have to use the same strategy we used for Amazon to find the selling price on the Barnes and Noble website. For this, we need to perform the following steps:

1. Find the URL for each ISBN
2. Find a way to scrape the selling price

The URL that can be used for Barnes and Noble is `http://www.barnesandnoble.com/s/ISBN`, where **ISBN** is the ISBN value, for example, `http://www.barnesandnoble.com/s/1904811590`.

Now, we have to find the selling price from the page. The page at Barnes and Noble will have the selling price listed in a `div` tag with the `price` class (highlighted) in the following screenshot:

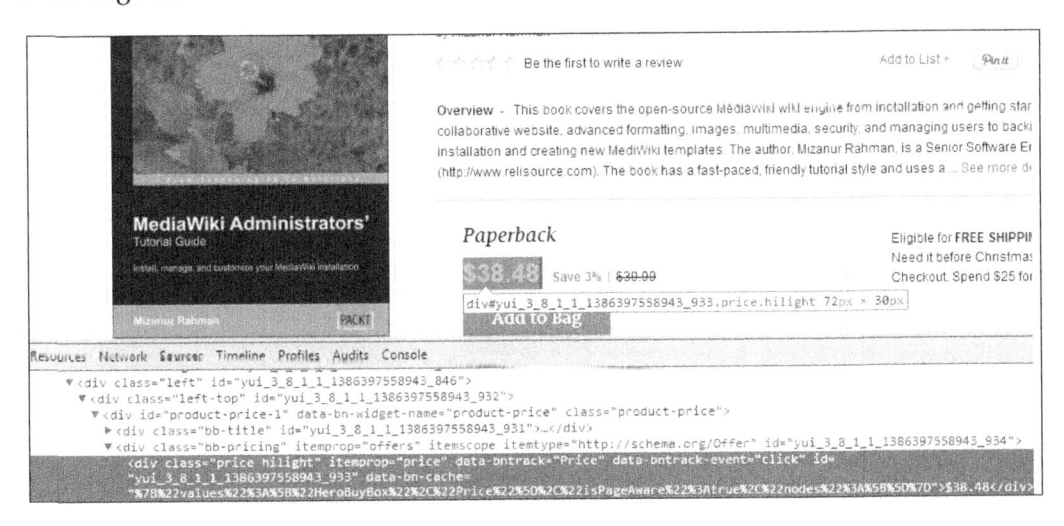

Creating a Web Scraper

We can find the selling price from Barnes and Noble using the following code:

```
def get_sellingprice_barnes(isbn):
  url_forbarnes = http://www.barnesandnoble.com/s/
  url_for_isbn_inbarnes = url_forbarnes+isbn
  page = urllib2.urlopen(url_for_isbn_inbarnes,"lxml")
  soup_barnes = BeautifulSoup(page,"lxml")
  page.close()
  selling_price_tag = soup_barnes.find('div',class_="price
    hilight")
  if selling_price_tag:
    print ("Barnes Price"+selling_price_tag.string)
```

The entire code for creating a web scrapper would be available at the code bundle

> The previous scraper can be freely download from the library

Summary

In this chapter, we created a sample scraper using Beautiful Soup. We used the search and navigation methods of Beautiful Soup to get information from packtpub.com, amazon.com, and barnesandnoble.com.

Index

Symbols

.children attribute 58
.contents attribute 57
.descendants attribute 58
.next_sibling attribute 62
.parent attribute 60
.parents attribute 61
.previous_sibling attribute 62
.string attribute 59
.strings attribute 60

A

append() method
  using 71, 75

B

Beautiful Soup
  encoding 88
  formatted printing 93
  installation, verifying 13
  installing 7
  installing, in Linux 7
  installing, in Windows 10
  navigation 53
  output 93
  output encoding 90
  output formatters 95
  searching 27
  search methods 27
  TreeBuilders 19
  unformatted printing 94
  using, without installation 12, 13

Beautiful Soup installation, in Linux
  easy_install, used 9
  package manager, used 8, 9
  performing 7, 8
  pip, used 9
Beautiful Soup installation, in Windows
  performing 10
  Python path, verifying 10, 11
  setup.py, used 12
BeautifulSoup object
  creating 15
  creating, for XML parsing 18
  creating, from file-like object 16, 17
  creating, from string 16
  features argument 19

C

clear() method
  using 79

D

decode() function 95
decompose() method
  using 77
descendants 56
direct children 56

E

easy_install 9
encode() method 91, 95
extract() method
  using 78

F

features argument 19-22
file-like object
  about 16
  BeautifulSoup object, creating from 16, 17
find_all() method, searching with
  about 37
  parameters, using 38, 39
  tertiary consumers, searching 37
find_all_previous() method 45
find() method 30
find() method, searching with
  regular expressions based search 32
  searching, functions used 35, 36
  searching methods, applying in combination 36
  tag attribute values based search 33
  tag, searching 31
  text, searching 32
find_next_sibling() method 43
find_next_siblings() method 43
find_parents() method 37
find_previous_sibling() method 44
find_previous_siblings() method 44
find_siblings() method 37
formatted printing 93
function formatter 99
functions, for content modifications
  insert_after() 80
  insert_before() 80
  replace_with() method 81
  unwrap() method 82
  wrap() method 82

G

get_bookurls() function 106
get_text()
  about 100
  using 100, 101

H

html5lib parser
  using 21
HTML document
  encoding, specifying 89, 90

html formatter 98
html.parser
  using 21

I

insert_after() method 80
insert() method
  using 73
installation
  Beautiful Soup 7

L

limit parameter, find_all() method 38
Linux
  Beautiful Soup, installing 7
lxml parser
  using 21

M

minimal formatter 98

N

NavigableString object 24, 53
navigating down
  about 55
  child tag name, using 55
  predefined attributes, using 56
  special attributes 59
navigating sideways, to siblings
  .next_sibling attribute 62
  .previous_sibling attribute 62
navigating up
  about 60
  .parent attribute 60
  .parents attribute 61
navigation, Beautiful Soup
  about 53, 54
  navigating down 55
  navigating sideways to siblings 61
  navigating to next and previous objects parsed 63
  navigating up 60
new tag
  adding, append() method used 72

adding, new_tag() method used 71
creating, new_tag() method used 71
new div tag, adding to li tag 73
new producer, adding using new_tag() and append() 71
new_tag() method
 using 71
next sibling
 searching for 44
None formatter 99

O

output encoding 90, 91
output formatters
 about 95-97
 function formatter 99
 html formatter 98
 minimal formatter 98
 None formatter 99

P

parameters, find_all() method
 limit parameter 38
pip 9
predefined attributes, for navigating down
 about 56
 .children attribute 58
 .contents attribute 57
 descendants 56
 .descendants attribute 58
 direct children 56
prettify() method 91-94
previous sibling
 searching for 45
Python Package Index (PyPI) 9

R

replace_with() method 81

S

searching, in Beautiful Soup
 about 27
 find_all() method used 37
 find() method used 28, 29
 next sibling, searching 44
 parent tags, searching 40
 previous sibling, searching 45
 siblings, searching 42, 44
 tags, searching 40
searching methods
 about 27
 used, for scraping information from web page 46-50
searching, with find()
 first producer, finding 29, 30
 performing 28, 29
setup.py script
 using 12
siblings
 searching for 42-44
soup.original_encoding 89
string contents, modifying
 about 73
 .string attribute, used 74
 strings, adding using .append() method 75
 strings, adding using insert() method 76
 strings, adding using new_string() method 76
str() method 95

T

tag attribute values based search, find() method used
 about 33
 CSS class based search 35
 custom attributes based search 34
 first primary consumer, finding 33
Tag modifying, Beautiful Soup used
 attribute value, adding 69
 attribute values, modifying 68
 attribute value, updating 68
 name property, modifying 66-68
 new tag, adding 71
 tag attributes, deleting 70
Tag object
 about 22
 accessing, from BeautifulSoup 22
 attributes 23
 name 23

tags
   contents, deleting using Beautiful Soup 79
   deleting, from HTML document 77
   parent tags, searching for 40, 41
   producer, deleting using decompose() 77
   producer, deleting using extract() 78
   searching for 40
TreeBuilders 19

U

unformatted printing 94
UnicodeDammit library 89
unicode() method 94
unwrap() method 83
UTF-8 87
UTF-8 encoding 89

W

website scraper
   book details, finding 107-109
   book details, getting 103
   creating 103, 106
   pages containing list of books, finding 104-106
   selling price, getting from Barnes and Noble 111
   selling price, searching on Amazon 109, 110
wrap() method 82

Thank you for buying
Getting Started with Beautiful Soup

About Packt Publishing

Packt, pronounced 'packed', published its first book "*Mastering phpMyAdmin for Effective MySQL Management*" in April 2004 and subsequently continued to specialize in publishing highly focused books on specific technologies and solutions.

Our books and publications share the experiences of your fellow IT professionals in adapting and customizing today's systems, applications, and frameworks. Our solution based books give you the knowledge and power to customize the software and technologies you're using to get the job done. Packt books are more specific and less general than the IT books you have seen in the past. Our unique business model allows us to bring you more focused information, giving you more of what you need to know, and less of what you don't.

Packt is a modern, yet unique publishing company, which focuses on producing quality, cutting-edge books for communities of developers, administrators, and newbies alike. For more information, please visit our website: www.packtpub.com.

About Packt Open Source

In 2010, Packt launched two new brands, Packt Open Source and Packt Enterprise, in order to continue its focus on specialization. This book is part of the Packt Open Source brand, home to books published on software built around Open Source licences, and offering information to anybody from advanced developers to budding web designers. The Open Source brand also runs Packt's Open Source Royalty Scheme, by which Packt gives a royalty to each Open Source project about whose software a book is sold.

Writing for Packt

We welcome all inquiries from people who are interested in authoring. Book proposals should be sent to author@packtpub.com. If your book idea is still at an early stage and you would like to discuss it first before writing a formal book proposal, contact us; one of our commissioning editors will get in touch with you.

We're not just looking for published authors; if you have strong technical skills but no writing experience, our experienced editors can help you develop a writing career, or simply get some additional reward for your expertise.

PySide GUI Application Development

ISBN: 978-1-84969-959-4   Paperback: 140 pages

Develop more dynamic and robust GUI applications using an open source cross-platform UI framework

1. Designed for beginners to help them get started with GUI application development
2. Develop your own applications by creating customized widgets and dialogs
3. Written in a simple and elegant structure to help you easily understand how to program various GUI components

Python Data Visualization Cookbook

ISBN: 978-1-78216-336-7   Paperback: 280 pages

Over 60 recipes that will enable you to learn how to create attractive visualizations using Python's most popular libraries

1. Learn how to set up an optimal Python environment for data visualization
2. Understand the topics such as importing data for visualization and formatting data for visualization
3. Understand the underlying data and how to use the right visualizations

Please check **www.PacktPub.com** for information on our titles

CherryPy Essentials
Rapid Python Web Application Development

ISBN: 978-1-90481-184-8　　　Paperback: 272 pages

Design, develop, test, and deploy your Python web applications easily

1. Walks through building a complete Python web application using CherryPy 3
2. The CherryPy HTTP:Python interface
3. Use CherryPy with other Python libraries
4. Design, security, testing, and deployment

Mobile First Design with HTML5 and CSS3

ISBN: 978-1-84969-646-3　　　Paperback: 122 pages

Roll out rock-solid, responsive mobile first designs quickly and reliably

1. Make websites that will look great and be usable on almost any device that displays web pages
2. Learn best practices for responsive design
3. Discover how to make designs that will be lean and fast on small screens without sacrificing a tablet or desktop experience

Please check www.PacktPub.com for information on our titles

Made in the USA
Middletown, DE
22 December 2020